SOME
CEMETERY RECORDS
OF
ABBEVILLE COUNTY,
SOUTH CAROLINA

CLEAR~
FIELD

Reprinted for
Clearfield Company, Inc. by
Genealogical Publishing Co., Inc.
Baltimore, Maryland
1993

NOTE

THE RECORDS appearing on the following pages were copied by the WPA—in a slightly different form—from tombstones in three cemeteries in Abbeville County, South Carolina: Melrose Cemetery, Episcopal Churchyard, and Long Canes Cemetery. The WPA transcripts, made in the 1930s, are now in the South Caroliniana Library, University of South Carolina, with whose kind permission this present condensed version is made available. The tombstone inscriptions, as given here, refer to persons who died between 1795 and 1936 and generally contain dates of birth and death and the names of immediate family members. While this work does not purport to cover all the cemeteries in Abbeville County, it does represent all of the records gathered by the WPA for this particular county.

MELROSE CEMETERY

Davis Marcus Keller b 4-17-1870 d 2-8-1919

Susan Elizabeth Hotzclaw w W. W. Keller b Washington, Ga.
  6-7-1850 d Abbeville, SC 5-10-1924

W. W. Keller b Abbeville, SC 5-10-1924

J. B. Davis b 1901 d 1934

Cora Horton Davis b 1901 d 1919

Mary E. Davis b 3-15-1863 d 2-6-1926

J. L. Wilson b 3-23-1876 d 12-13-1925

Ernest Shaw s B. L. & Lillian Shaw b. 12-29-1905 d 10-25-1925

Hugh Green b Ireland Age 72 Years

Mary Blanchet w W. M. Grant b 12-1-1871 d 12-24-1923

Kenneth Brogden s A. L. & A. Brogden b 10-5-1921 d 10-6-1921

Lawrence N. Finley b 5-2-1897 d 2-3-1927

Nancy E. Finley w Jim Finley b 4-19-1875 d 4-18-1923

Belle Sorrow b 11-18-1874 d 11-15-1930

Parks E. Sorrow b 9-16-1898 d 2-3-1922

J. Earnest Simpson b 11-4-1888 d 4-20-1917

Curtis H. Hall s A. L. & Ada Hall b 5-11-1923 d 2-25-1924

Mary Lee Creswell dau Mr & Mrs J A. Creswell 5-31-1929

Doris Francis dau Mr & Mrs J. A. Creswell b 5-6-1931 d 6-12-1932 '

Jane Bell Creswell b 11-11-1869 d 12-30-1929

Johnnie Lourie Creswell b 6-26-1894 d 9-12-1917

Huey Hunsucker d 8-10-1919 Aged 27 Years

T. M. Horton d 11-23-1929 Age 67 Years

Crattie Lue Horton w T. M. Horton d 5-4-1914 Aged 44 Years

MELROSE CEMETERY

William Nixon b 12-25-1864 d 2-4-1923

Blanche dau C. M. & Lucile Williams 3-7-1923

James H. Burdett b 10-23-1848 d 8-28-1927 Confederate Vet.

Vemmie White b 1862 d 1930

M. C. Beasley 7-17-1917

S. Beasley b 7-15-1883 d 3-21-1917

Robert s J. M. & G. D. Graham b 11-20-1915 d 6-3-1917

Roland Kirby b 1898 d 1928

Marion dau J. R. & M. O. Kirby b 1921 d 1921

Maud Hinton w J. H. Hinton b 6-25-1891 d 5-26-1919

May Hinton w J. H. Hinton b 10-16-1862 d 4-28-1913

Lina Lee dau E. H. & M. B. Harrison b 7-9-1902 d 8-19-1903

Carrie Lueviena Banks w W. E. Banks b 9-14-1867 d 1-5-1910

Beular Hortense Banks w W. E. Banks b 9-3-1883

Infant Son of R. O. & S. E. Thompson 7-30-1905 to 7-31-1905

Jason L. Simpson b 1840 d 1916

John R. Wilson b 2-28-1840 d 2-26-1917

William R. Wilson b 4-3-1875 d 10-18-1918 Woodmen of World

A. H. Willis b 4-22-1848 d 8-30-1906

Japhos R. s A. H. & S. L. Willis b 8-25-1893 d 8-15-1902

Fannie E. Willis w W. R. Wilson b 8-28-1885 d 6-3-1911

Ben S. Willis b 6-27-1891 d 6-9-1925

Billy s W. C. & A. E. Edmonds b 8-3-1916 d 6-4-1918

Virginia dau J. L. & E. R. Govin b 8-28-1908 d 7-3-1909

Samuel A. Willis b 3-19-1862 d 2-18-1917

Infant Son of J. F. & Mattie Edmonds 8-9-1890

Daniel Brunson s J. F. & Mattie B. Edmonds b 4-4-1904 d 8-17-1904

Infant Son of J. F. & Mattie B. Edmonds 10-28-1907

2

Samuel Dudley s J. F. & Mattie B. Edmonds b 9-13-1909
  d 5-4-1910

Infant of Mr & Mrs W. H. M. Gunter b & d 6-25-1906

Infant Dau of Mr & Mrs G. B. Cox b & d 2-23-1917

Curtis H. s A. L. & Ada Hall b 5-11-1923 d 2-25-1924

J. Earnest Simpson b 11-4-1888 d 4-20-1917

John Frith b 1-2-1846 d 12-31-1927

Matilda Frith w John Frith b 9-15-1851 d 5-12-1923

Fannie Finley b 1881 d 3-29-1915

Ruth V. dau P. L. & C. C. Blanchett b 6-20-1913 d 9-28-1914

Magie Lee dau P. L. & C. C. Blanchett b 2-22-1906 d 5-10-1921

Ansel A. s P. L. & Cleo Blanchett b 7-5-1908 d 3-21-1933
  Enlisted US Navy 2-4-1925

P. L. Blanchett b 4-27-1872

Cleo C. Blanchett b 7-28-1881 d 8-5-1935

J. A. Blanchett d 9-13-1919 Aged 48 Years

Mary E. C. dau S. H. & Katie New d 4-23-1911 Aged 22 Years

Tommie Allen s M. B. & C. C. New b 7-28-1907 d 9-10-1908

Mrs. Katie New w S. A. New d 4-27-1927 Aged 60 Years

Ralph s J. M. & M. Carroll 1914

Katie Carroll w J. M. Carroll b 6-13-1870 d 11-13-1907

Bennie F. s J. M. & M. Carroll d 6-4-1920 Aged 9 Years

Mary E. Finley b 12-17-1919 d 3-29-1914

James s W. L. & Ola Clark b 1-29-1906 d 7-24-1909

Ola Clark b 8-12-1883 d 6-28-1914

Charlie Mahaffey b 3-3-1910 d 8-12-1913

Two Little Grandchildren of J. D. & D. A. Mahaffey

Ethel May dau J. L. & L. S. Mahaffey b 11-3-1910 d 1-16-1911

O. L. Cann b 1-1-1845 d 1-19-1918

3

Mary E. Cann w O. L. Cann b 6-9-1845 d 4-15-1913

Euna Ethelene dau E. P. & E. M. Woolbright b 11-16-1920
d 2-20-1921

Watson J. Clark b 10-22-1894 d 3-9-1921

John L. Clark b 1-9-1874 d 5-11-1930

James Andrew Blanchett b 6-10-1879 d 10-30-1918

Allen Kidd b 6-18-1900 d 10-31-1918

Ralph s M. B. & N. C. Cann b 4-4-1901 d 5-16-1913

Obie s W. T. & Alice Cann b 11-5-1908 d 11-15-1911

G. C. Dudley b 5-21-1870 d 8-25-1928

Mrs. E. M. Dudley w C. C. Dudley b 1-7-1877 d 9-10-1919

W. M. Blanchett b 2-10-1866 d 5-30-1921 Woodmen of World

Dorah Fowler b 1-10-1875 d 6-25-1935

Albert Sidney s H. S. & M. Corley b 3-17-1920 d 4-28-1920

John M. Jr. s J. M. & E. P. James b 3-3-1920 d 6-20-1920

Willie Ansel s J. M. & E. P. James b 7-5-1923 d 11-20-1928

William J. s J. M. & E. P. James b 6-18-1913 d 8-16-1913

Mary James w J. B. James d 3-13-1915 Aged 50 Years

Willie James b 5-28-1902 d 3-18-1913

J. B. James b 4-16-1863 d 7-1-1912

Mary F. Hamlin b 4-14-1840 d 6-25-1918

E. E. s R. L. & Sarah C. Williams b 2-15-1859 d 7-10-1920

E. Alvin s E. E. & A. H. Williams b 7-10-1892 d 3-14-1926

James Edward s E. A. & Leila Williams b 8-2-1917 d 10-15-1919

Eddie Alvin Jr. s E. A. & Leila Williams b 8-1-1915 d 4-19-1917

John T. s J. M. & Ida Wham b 10-18-1908 d 12-24-1909

Mary Helen dau J. M. & I. O. Wham b 3-8-1903 d 11-27-1911

Mary Bolick Harris b 4-17-1874 d 8-3-1914

MELROSE CEMETERY

James Bolick s W. H. & M. B. Harris b 6-25-1908 d 7-31-1909

Bertha L. Landrum w W. W. Landrum b 11-11-1861 d 4-22-1908

Edith L. Leach w W. T. Stephens b 10-3-1893 d 10-17-1924

Mary E. Stephens w W. G. Stephens b 2-2-1860 d 10-10-1932

William G. Stephens b 6-2-1865 d 9-17-1911

Infant Dau of Samuella Shaw & Henry Gilliam b 7-29-1912
    d 9-2-1912

Infant Dau of Samuella Shaw & Henry Gilliam b 4-5-1918
    d 4-11-1918

Cora M. Raines w J. C. Raines b 5-15-1864 d 2-1-1902

Mary Lee dau J. C. & Cora M. Raines b 1-26-1902 d 8-16-1902

Jas. Bratton s J. C. & C. M. Raines b 3-15-1894 d 9-16-1900
    & Infant Sister 3-18-1900

Mary E. dau G. W. & M. E. Lomax b 5-26-1895 d 10-10-1909

Julia dau G. W. & M. E. Lomax b 5-1-1903 d 6-1-1905

George W. Lomax b 6-25-1866 d 10-30-1904

M. Eliza McIlwain w George W. Lomax b 9-19-1868 d 3-30-1907

David K. s G. W. & M. E. Lomax b 7-23-1897 d 5-14-1899

Kate Estelle Delph dau Marie Louise Pelletier & Robert
    Jasper Delph b 9-1860 d 3-1927

William Andrew s Marie Louise Pelletier & James Fuller
    Lyon b 10-13-1867 d 9-29-1930

J. Fuller Lyon b 4-1-1842 d 11-5-1920 Co. H 19th SCV

Marie Louise Pelletier w J. Fuller Lyon b 1841 d 1895

Jefferson Hayne McDill b 8-31-1861 d 4-3-1912

William Andrew McDill s Jasphere Virginia Delph & Jefferson
    Haynie McDill b 12-1896 d 7-1925

Robert Grier Hemphill s Robert & Eugenia Hemphill m Jessie
    Culver 8-3-1910 b 2-7-1885 d 6-19-1930. Honor Graduate
    College Charleston 1903, Irrigation Engineer 1906 to death.

Robert Reid Hemphill b 5-3-1840 d 12-28-1908 Member Co. B 7th
    SCV & Orr's Reg Rifles, First Manassas, Member Wallace House
    Legislator, State Senator & Clerk of Senate 1876-1908.

Gottlob A. Neuffer Jr. b 11-30-1889 d 11-27-1933
American U.S. Legion 1st Lieut. Machine Gun Co. 118
Inf 30th Div, A.E.F. in France 5-8-1819 to 12-18-1918

Annie Hemphill w Dr. G. A. Neuffer b 2-6-1871 d 4-23-1899

Maria Louise dau C. V. & J. R. Neuffer b 10-18-1907
d 6-12-1908

Infant dau of Dr. & Mrs Neuffer b 9-7-1892

Henry Hemphill Sign b 11-4-1895 d 5-17-1901

Henry R. Sign b 1-1875 d 3-1911

Martin Teague Coleman b 9-25-1895 d 10-6-1895

Infant son of J. C. & S. C. Butler b & d 12-22-1895

Sarah Emma Butler b 9-9-1863 d 12-24-1899

Infant dau of J. C. & S. P. Butler d 4-28-1903 Aged 3 Days

James Chalmers Butler b 11-21-1846 d 12-24-1904

J. F. Thornton b 3-15-1866 d 5-25-1912 Woodmen of World

Eva Dorn dau W. L. & Ella Power b 7-10-1915 d 4-7-1917

J. Earnest Cheatham b 1878 d 1920

Janie Britt w R. B. Cheatham b 6-26-1876 d 11-20-1924

Infant child of R. B. & J. B. Cheatham 10-6-1901

Infant son of R. B. & Janie B. Cheatham b 4-30-1911
d 5-4-1911

Frederic Minshall b Piedmont, W. Va. 8-31-1871 d Abbeville,
SC 3-5-1912

John Thompson Clinkscales b 1-7-1863 d 12-10-1912

Sudie Nance Clinkscales b 6-17-1864 d 11-29-1912

Ruth Edwards adopted dau John T. & Sudie Clinkscales
b 5-8-1902 d 12-5-1912

William G. Riley b 2-1-1852 d 6-14-1913 Chief of Police
31 years

Mamie Lou Fulmer b 4-20-1893 d 7-21-1934

Lula Blackwell Hutchison w W. F. Clary b 11-27-1872
d 2-15-1910

MELROSE CEMETERY

Eva Smith w T. A. Able b 9-2-1890 d 8-8-1929

William Samuel s Mr & Mrs T. A. Able 1934

Milton Bradley Reese b 8-9-1877 d 2-18-1932

Nell Reese w G. R. Martz b 11-19-1882 d 1-2-1926

Henry Dodson Reese b 12-25-1852 d 7-16-1924

Ella Eugenia Bradley w H. D. Reese b 11-30-1859 d 1-19-1910

Corrie M. Killingsworth b 12-9-1869 d 4-2-1933

Percy James Leach b 1869 d 1930

Samuel F. s Dr. & Mrs S. F. Killingsworth b 10-6-1902
    d 6-26-1903

James s S. F. & C. K. Killingsworth b 7-19-1907 d 12-21-1909

Infant son of W. R. & E. F. Speed 11-3-1919

Lucius L. Owens b 2-16-1867 d 7-15-1901

Rev. Jesse M. Owens b 3-12-1844 d 9-13-1893 Member North
    Conference

Marthena C. Owens w Rev. J. M. Owens b 4-29-1846 d 5-18-1916

Althea dau P. B. & A. O. Speed b 3-25-1899 d 8-25-1901

Preston Brooks s Ezekiel & Julia Baker Speed b 1-11-1858
    d 1-11-1928

Preston Brooks Speed b 11-29-1891 d 2-26-1933

Howard Owens Speed b 11-12-1894 d 5-17-1933

Ann Miller Stark 11-10-1933

Samuel Brown b 1836 d 1908

C. A. Baskin b 4-11-1881 d 8-26-1931

Claude Clinkscales Gambrell, M.D. b 3-2-1872 d 1-13-1925

James Robert Grubb b 11-13-1873 d 6-16-1932

Virginia Gambrell w Walter S. Zimmerman, Deluth Minnesota
    b 2-3-1888 d 11-12-1917

Ellen Wright Cason b 12-3-1902 d 11-16-1909

Eliza Cassandra Clinkscales w John M. Gambrell b 1846 d 1922

MELROSE CEMETERY

John Marion Gambrell b 1846 d 1928

Marion S. s George C. & Mae McLaughen b 1905 d 1933

Milford Clinkscales b 1-8-1906 d 11-18-1928

Lamar Clinkscales b 1-12-1858 d 12-27-1915

Wm. H. Austin d 6-24-1917 Aged 7 Years

Edward M. Bond b 11-12-1870 d 9-10-1932

Cornelia J. Bond b 11-5-1874

Mary Agnes dau Claude & Lillie Campbell b 9-12-1930
     d 1-17-1935

Betty J. Timmons b 2-2-1924 d 5-3-1934

Thomas B. Argo b 1884 d 1934

Mary Fowler Argo b 1884 d 1919

Dolly Blanchett Cann b 1877

Thos. Lester Cann b 1877 d 1921

Mary I. Godfrey d 10-9-1920 Aged 45 Years

George W. Godfrey b 8-14-1876 d 3-31-1929 Woodmen of World

G. Frank Godfrey b 7-3-1899 d 12-22-1924

Sarah Harris Haigler b 8-17-1870 d 6-18-1920

Sarah Haigler Shuman b 10-10-1840 d 11-26-1910

John Tompkins Mabry s John M. & Rebecca McWilliams Mabry
     b 8-12-1890 d 12-23-1914

Nancy Allena dau John M. & Rebecca McWilliams Mabry
     b 1-12-1897 d 7-25-1933

Agnes dau George W. & Ann Batson b 2-10-1914 d 6-14-1934

Earl Gilleland s B. H. & E. G. Cason b 3-23-1907 d 5-28-1907

Helena E. Gramer w G. W. Gilleland b 3-12-1886 d 11-10-1913

Alexander W. Clark b 4-18-1846 d 4-22-1918

Thurston T. Clark b 2-17-1884 d 3-2-1917

Granville Beal b 1-6-1854 d 10-3-1912

8

MELROSE CEMETERY

Elda Bourquin w Granville Beal b 1861 d 1917

Isidora Hicks w Joseph Hicks b 1850 d 1926

Joseph Hicks b 1849 d 1929

Pearl Bates w Henry Hill DuPre b 12-17-1890 d 11-15-1918

James E. Young d 4-2-1928 Georgia VT 14.8 Inf 37 Div

Kinard L. s W. A. & M. G. McCurry b 3-26-1901 d 8-28-1902

Schalon A. s W. A. & M. G. McCurry b 4-11-1899 d 6-10-1900

J. B. Baker b 1885 d 1920

Infant Babes of A. B. & L. M. Hamlin Jr. b 2-6-1902
    d 2-6 & 2-7-1902

George M. Gable b 7-6-1907 d 7-26-1928

Milton Jackson Hodges b 6-26-1892 d 5-8-1932

Glenn B. Baskin b 10-18-1885 d 4-28-1932

Mattia S. McCurry w H. E. McCurry b 3-17-1869 d 10-25-1907

Infant of H. E. & M. S. McCurry b 9-8-1899 d 12-17-1899

Lilla I. McCurry b 10-20-1870 d 2-17-1906

Margaret Malilda Campbell w John W. McCurry b 2-9-1832
    d 1-16-1918 m 1-20-1854

John W. McCurry b 1-15-1829 d 7-14-1917 CoI 14 SC Inf CSA

Mary Elender dau W. B. & M. E. Patterson b 4-17-1906 d 7-19-1906

William B. Patterson b 9-12-1863 d 4-13-1914 Woodmen of World

Mary E. McCurry w W. B. Patterson b 5-2-1866 d 5-4-1906

William S. Taggart b 2-6-1861 d 1-17-1923

William R. Pennal b 1-18-1883 d 8-9-1917

Wynona V. dau Mr & Mrs C. F. Martin b 9-10-1926 d 10-3-1931

Doris dau Mr & Mrs C. F. Martin b 5-10-1923 d 12-6-1931

Mary E. dau W. M. & Collie Langley b 10-18-1909 d 6-20-1910

Jack Keith s William Meadors & Collie P. Langley b 5-18-1911
    d 9-4-1913

MELROSE CEMETERY

Wilma Whatley dau William Meadors & Collie P. Langley
b 7-11-1913 d 7-9-1914

Norma C. Langley b 10-4-1918 d 5-16-1933

Carrie K. Langley w J. B. Langley b 4-1-1860 d 7-24-1911

Edmund B. s J. B. & C. K. Langley b 3-12-1888 Killed in
France 10-31-1918

Norman H. Langley b 12-3-1893 d 2-26-1928 Ex-Lieut U.S.
Air Service World War Veteran

Thedore s C. H. & L. S. Douglas b 4-26-1912 d 6-7-1914

Capt. Elbridge R. Clinkscales b 8-31-1839 d 3-31-1918
1861-1865

J. A. Jr. Youngest s John A. & Beulah C. Nance b 2-26-1900
d 1-19-1919

Doris dau C. I. & F. E. Young b 8-2-1926 d 5-20-1927

Charlie Young b 11-20-1893 d 4-4-1932

Mary Adline dau J. A. & M. A. Porter d 11-29-1926 Aged 7 Years

William Robert s J. A. & M. A. Porter d 2-14-1926 Aged 7 Weeks

Jack Jr. s S. J. & E. G. Woolbright b 6-3-1921 d 10-22-1922

John J. Long b 3-26-1855 d 11-27-1926

Lula Long b 10-6-1860 d 2-2-1928

M. Cornelia dau E. V. & Addie Canfield d 9-17-1926 Aged 6 Months

William T. Edwards b 1859 d 1926

Bettie Creswell w William T. Edwards b 1867 d 1933

Wallace Martin 1928

C. H. Edmunds b 1860 d 1935

Mary Harling w C. H. Edmunds b 1859 d 1933

Mary A. McCaslan w B. S. Barnwell b 1842 d 1925

B. S. Barnwell b 1834 d 1907

Mary Barnwell w Wyatt Aiken b Abbeville, S.C. 10-11-1872
d Washington, D.C. 4-14-1904

Wyatt Aiken b 12-14-1863 d 2-6-1923 Adut. 1st S.C. Vol
Spanish Amer. War Representative in Congress 1903-1917

Patrick H. McCaslan b 6-16-1848 d 6-19-1924 Woodmen of World

Margaret Susan McCaslan b 11-13-1834 d 10-6-1913

William M. Jr. s W. M. & J. E. Barnwell b 7-30-1913
  d 6-10-1915

James Coke Klugh b 4-30-1857 d 10-12-1911 Practiced Law
  15 years. Judge S.C. Courts 20 years. Member M.E. Church

Infant dau J. C. & C. B. Klugh 4-10-1908

Charles B. s J. C. & C. B. Klugh b 6-9-1905 d 5-27-1906

Caroline dau J. C. & C. B. Klugh b 9-5-1900 d 6-3-1902

Infant dau J. C. & C. B. Klugh 5-10-1898

Infant dau J. C. & C. B. Klugh 5-12-1899

William Washington Hunter

Nancy Glasgow Hunter

Joseph Franklin Hunter

William Andrew Hunter, M.D.

Sarah Elizabeth Hunter

Margaret Jane Hunter

Henry Edmund Hunter

Mary Katherine Hunter

John Edward Hunter   Confederate Veteran

John Howard Moore b 1-9-1876 d 8-26-1927 Served Abbeville
Co. in House 1911-1918 In Senate 1918-1927

Sallie Sue dau J. O. & L. V. Seal b 9-25-1922 d 5-8-1924

Same Adams b 5-7-1893 d 6-1-1919 H.D.Q. Co. 53 Inf 6 Div

Claude E. s G. P. & E. V. Hughes b 12-18-1891 d 10-11-1918
  Batt D 316 Coast Art. 81 Div

John Lyon b 3-19-1841 d 4-1-1906

Margaret Elizabeth Lyon w John Lyon b 12-4-1847 d 7-14-1915

James Foster Bradley b 2-2-1871 d 1-20-1916 Woodmen of World

Infant dau H. E. & M. B. Pressly 1-16-1916

11

Margaret B. dau V. D. & Lora Thomas b 4-12-1915 d 5-17-1917

Louise H. dau R. S. & C. L. Ellis b 10-26-1902 d 7-6-1914

Jim Parthemas b 11-8-1889 d 11-19-1918

William Edgar Jr. s W. E. & Lucy Owen b 7-28-1901 d 4-13-1917

James F. Clinkscales b 1859 d 1922

Ella A. Kay w James F. Clinkscales b 1864 d 1923

Verna Clinkscales w John T. Stokes b 12-6-1890 d 2-11-1932

John Franklin Clinkscales b 1-7-1910 d 5-29-1914

Ida T. DuPre w G. W. Carroll b 6-3-1866 d 10-23-1917

Geo. W. Carroll b 1-16-1866 d 3-9-1934

John W. Carroll b 11-9-1892 d 3-19-1931

Lewis Blount Jr. b 6-21-1880 d 11-6-1918

Ruby V. Blount b 9-27-1888 d 11-9-1918

Linda Higgason w J. A. Wilson b 7-21-1873 d 11-22-1919

Deney Simpson b 4-7-1907 d 9-14

Blanche Inez dau M. B. & C. C. New b 5-16-1919 d 7-25-1922

James Robert Martin b 1-21-1934 d 1-7-1935

EPISCOPAL CHURCHYARD

Jehu Foster Marshall and wife Elizabeth DeBruhl Marshall
  Elizabeth DeBruhl Marshall b 9-4-1923 d 12-23-1868
  Jehu Foster Marshall Col. First Regt. Rifles SC Vol
    fell at Second Battle Manassas b 8-28-1817 d 8-28-1862
  Served thro the Mexican War, elected State Senator for
  Abbeville Dist.

Robert Wesley Wilson d 1866 Aged 25 Years

Mrs. Mary Wilson d 1868 Aged 56 Years

Hugh Wilson b 1838 d 1917

P. J. Grant

M. P. Morgan

Soldier

Capt. P. Thomas

A. F. Marion   Calhoun County, AL

William Dixon

Charlott Haskell d 12-2-1836 Aged 1 Mon 3 Days

Charles Thomson Haskell d 12-27-1874 Aged 72 Years 10 Mon
   Erected by his 6 surviving sons.

Sophia Lovell w Charles Thomas Haskell dau Langdon Cleves
   b 7-1-1809 d 7-30-1881

Charles Thomson Haskell b 3-28-1835 Fell in defense of
   Charleston Harbour 7-10-1863 Capt. Co D 1st Regt. SC
   Regulars CSA

William Thomson Haskell bro of Charles Thomson Haskell
   b 12-11-1837 Fell in front of Battle of Gettysburg 7-2-1863
   Capt. Co H 1st Regt. SCV, Gregg's Brigade A.N. Va. Served in
   battles of Sumter, Vienna, Mechanicsville, Cold Harbor, Frasers
   Farm, Malvern Hill, 2nd Manissas, Ox Hill, Harpers Ferry, Sharps-
   burg, Shepardstown, Fredericksburg, Chancellorsville and
   Commanding Battalion of Skermishers.

Allen Wardlaw Haskell b 10-28-1863 d 7-26-1926

Nanita Perry dau John Samuel & Amelia Churchell Norwood
   b 7-25-1882 d 12-11-1901

Amelia Walker dau John Samuel & Amelia Churchell Norwood
   b 11-25-1899 d 10-25-1901

David Walter Thomas b 8-4-1850 d 1-27-1930

E. Annie dau Thomas Walter & Elizabeth H. K. Thomas
   b. 7-15-1841 d 6-2-1899

Elizabeth Hamilton Kirk Thomas w Thomas Walter Thomas
   whose body lies buried at Long Cane d 7-18-1868 Aged 57 Years

Dr. James W. Thomas b 10-12-1832 d 10-15-1899

Mary Cheatham Thomas w James Walter Thomas b 9-26-1841 d 4-6-1916

Jas. Walter Thomas b 5-28-1864 d 5-13-1865

Grace Allerton Thomas b 4-11-1878 d 5-2-1899

Willie Thomas b 11-29-1876 d 7-26-1877

Willie Walter Brooks b 3-17-1888 d 3-16-1905

Leunie Walter Thomas Brooks b 2-1862 d 6-1921

Eunice Perrin Gass b 1-20-1885 Aged 3 Mon 9 Days

James O'Neill s B. W. & F. O. Barwiell b 5-23-1826 d 12-29-1877

Mary Noble w Aug. W. Smith b 11-1861 d 12-1898

Margaret dau A. W. & M. N. Smith 8-7-1898

Infant dau of Augustus M. & Sarah M. Smith b 3-2-1859 d 3-3-1859

Roselie Ella dau Augustus M. & Sarah M. Smith d 7-26-1859
    Aged 16 Mon 16 Days

Augustus Marshall Smith b 10-22-1827 d Richmond, Va 6-30-1862
    of wound received in battle of Gaines Mill. From Private to
    Lieut. Colonel of first Gregg's Regt SC Vol

Sarah Margert Wardlaw w Augustus Smith dau David Lewis Wardlaw
    b 9-27-1839 d 2-26-1911

Ernest s Augustus Marshall Smith & Sarah Margaret Wardlaw
    b 7-11-1860 d 4-22-1888

Lewis Wardlaw Smith

Margaret Wardlaw Parker d 7-27-1870 Aged 10 Mon 19 Days

Eller Elizabeth Second child William H. & Lucian G. Parker
    b 5-16-1858 d 8-2-1859

Sarah Allen dau William H. & Lucia G. Parker b 11-10-1856
    d 3-19-1858

Rosalie Simkins Parker

Edward Frost Parker b 2-5-1860 d 10-2-1872

William Henry Parker s Thomas & Ellen Frost Parker b 1-1-1828
    d 2-7-1906

Lucea Garvey w William Henry Parker dau David Lewis & Sarah
    Allen Wardlaw b 4-22-1833 d 10-29-1897

Allen Wardlaw Parker b 6-16-1867 d 8-3-1891

James Alexander Norwood b 8-1-1810 d 12-7-1874

Sarah Hester w James Alexander Norwood b 7-7-1817 d 1-16-1887

Martha Maria Calhoun b 8-6-1870 d 12-7-1894

Willie Glover Norwood b 8-18-1845 d 6-8-1875

James Alexander s James A. & Sarah Norwood b 1-2-1850
d 11-15-1886

Lila Norwood b 11-19-1857 d 3-5-1901

James Perrin s E. R. & M. R. Lucas b 4-11-1896 d 4-15-1896.

Mamie N. Perrin w Edwin R. Lucas b 2-10-1875 d 4-23-1896

Thomas Parker b 11-10-1832 Fell at Battle of Secessionville
6-16-1862

Clarissa Annie Fleming Eldest child of Thomas & Margaretta
A. Parker b 1-2-1859 d 11-29-1862

Ellen Legare Parker Relict of Thomas Parker dau Rev. Thomas
& Elizabeth Frost of Charleston b 6-5-1797 d 4-11-1879

Edward Frost Parker b 4-6-1830 d 4-13-1888

Lisa DeVeaux w Thomas Fleming Parker dau William Parker
& Julia DeVeaux Foulke of Philadelphia b 3-8-1860 d 5-8-1902

Julia DeVeaux dau Thomas Fleming & Lisa DeVeaux Parker
b 3-27-1896 d 4-5-1896

William Campbell McGowan b 3-16-1858 d 2-27-1898

J. A. Calhoun Co G 2 SC Cav. CSA

Aurelia C. Rucker d 3-22-1899 Aged 65 Years

Sarah M. Calhoun w John A. Calhoun dau Williamson Norwood
b 5-18-1814 d 12-3-1891

John Alfred Calhoun s James & Sarah Calhoun m Sarah Mourin
Norwood b 1-8-1807 d 8-25-1874

Mary Norwood w William James Lomax dau of John A. & Sarah
N. Calhoun b 3-30-1834 d 4-6-1856

James Caldwell Calhoun d 5-27-1885 Aged 23 Years 10 Mon 20 Days

Robert Henry Baker b Selma, Ala. 7-4-1862 d Sumter, SC 12-17-1896

Corp. W. N. Calhoun Co D 7 SC Inf. CSA

Joseph Rucker d 2-12-1861 Aged 1 Year

Louisa Small b 7-20-1845 Aged 21 Years 29 Days

Mary Irwin sister of Louisa Small b 6-13-1857 Aged 8 Years
1 Mon 7 Days
Eva Enverdale Small sister of Louisa Small b 10-18-1855
Aged 17 Years 6 Mon

15

Emilie Washington Small sister of Louisa Small b 12-19-1859
Aged 7 Years 8 Mon 27 Days

James Townes Robertson b 8-19-1832 d 8-31-1905 Lieut Col.
Orr's Regt. of Rifles, McGowans Brigade CSA

Eugenia Miller w J. Townes Robertson b 10-11-1852 d 5-30-1894

Louis Robertson w J. A. Cheek b 10-14-1881 d 11-10-1912

John A. Cheek b 12-12-1877 d 12-29-1923

Louis Robertson dau J. A. & L. R. Cheek b 10-12-1904 d 5-5-1906

Mary W. Thomas w William C. Parker b 5-19-1846 d 6-7-1920

William Calhoun Parker b 2-7-1854 d 7-27-1875

Henry Hester Norwood b 12-8-1851 d 5-15-1902

Ellen Frost Parker w Henry H. Norwood b 9-10-1855 d 12-2-1933

Edward Parker, M.D. b 5-14-1823 d 10-5-1884

Eugenia G. Parker b 10-10-1825 d 5-20-1873

Thomas Drayton Parker b 9-7-1848 d 11-18-1879

Edward Eugene s Edwin & Eugenia Calhoun Parker b 9-2-1860
d 1-16-1888

Belle dau Edward & Mary Battrex Noble b 5-20-1852 d 12-9-1865

William Bratton s Edward & Mary Battrex Noble b 9-18-1864
d 7-5-1865

William Augustus Lee b 3-2-1826 d 10-23-1896

Charles Francis Lee b 5-15-1861 d 1-2-1897 When on a visit
from Kentucky to the home of his birth at Due West, SC

Ben Robert Augustus Lee b 2-17-1868 Killed by lightning near
Brevard, NC 7-15-1896. Rector of the Church of the Good
Sheppeard at Yorkville, SC.

John Jinkins Lee, M.D. b 3-22-1819 d 12-29-1876.

Agnes Baker Robertson b 1845 d 1901

J. William Robertson d 2-16-1881 Aged 4 Years 8 Mon 8 Days

John A. Hunter d 8-15-1868 Aged 51 Years

Sarah Posey w B. L. Posey d 7-13-1836 Leaving 7 children

B. L. Posey d 11-2-1843 in 54th Year

Martha A. Posey d 8-26-1844 in 19th Year

Dora dau Dr. A. W. & Elizabeth Lynch

Mrs. Mary Posey cons Benjamin V. Posey b 1760 d 1840
  Aged 80 Years Member Turkey Creek Baptist Church

N. H. Miller Jr. b 1-20-1852 d 2-23-1876 Aged 24 Years

Col. N. H. Miller b 6-9-1804 d 8-28-1855

Mary Yarbrough w Col. N. H. Miller b 4-12-1812 d 7-23-1893

William Yarbrough b 10-17-1769 d 9-10-1835

Mary Yarbrough w William Yarbrough b 7-17-1777 d 9-3-1835

Henry Latimer s T. L. & M. C. Cozby d 5-12-1879 Aged 1 Mon

Ann Martin dau John Wier b 11-1-1819 d 8-6-1842

William Richey b 10-1787 d 8-1819

Margaret D. Richey b 1-17-1819 d 12-19-1834

John Dunn d 9-6-1841 in 38th Year

Robert Richey b 3-2-1805 d 2-15-1848 Left wife & 2 children

Margaret Wier cons John Wier b 3-29-1794 d 11-27-1848
  Aged 54 Years 7 Mon 28 Days. Member Presbyterian Church
  35 years.

John Wier b 11-28-1849 Aged 67 Years 2 Mon 17 Days
  Member Presbyterian Church 35 years.

Unmarked graves of five adults are next to above.

Richard A. Hamilton d 2-11-1837 in 22nd Year

Thomas Alexander s James S. & Susan V. Wilson b 12-9-1832
  d 7-7-1834 Aged 18 Mon 23 Days

Alexander C. Hamilton b 9-28-1782 d 2-27-1835
  Aged 52 Years 5 Mon

Delphia Adelia w Capt, A. C. Hamilton d 11-7-1826 Aged 39 Years

Cathrine Hamilton Alston w Major James Alston dau Maj.
Andrew & Jane Hamilton b 11-25-1786 d 11-18-1877

Maj. James Alston b 11-16-1774 d 12-15-1850 Officer in
the first Seminole War.

Major Andrew Hamilton d 1-17-1835 in 95th Year
The name Major Hamilton is connected with almost the
whole of the Rev. history of the up country of SC. A
member Presbyterian Church.

Mrs. Jane Hamilton w Major Andrew Hamilton d 4-20-1826
in 86th Year

Albert Henry b 11-24-1879 d 5-3-1921

A. McIlwaine Henry b 2-15-1882 d 1-14-1919

A. Mc. Henry Jr. "Infant" d 1-16-1919

Sarah Ellen Hill w Francis Henry b 10-14-1843 d 4-16-1927

Francis Henry b 9-23-1843 d 3-23-1912

Frank s F & S. C. Henry d 8-3-1893 Aged 9 Years 7 Mon

John Thomson s Francis & S. E. Henry d 12-9-1877
Aged 13 Mon 12 Days

Anna H. Hill w Wm. Hill d 10-16-1880 Aged 73 Years (nearly)

Wm. Hill b County Antrim, Ireland 5-19-1805 d 1-14-1886

Andrew McIlwain b 5-29-1832 d 4-18-1865 in Va. while a
Soldier in the Confed. Army.

John W. Calvert b 3-18-1840 d 3-6-1870 Old Soldier

Sarah J. Hill w R. E. Hill b 8-26-1839 d 5-23-1872

Mary Thomson Hill w Robert E. Hill d 2-17-1885 Aged 34 Years
4 Mon 4 Days

Andrew M. Hamilton b 2-17-1808 d 3-19-1888

Mattie Ward w R. E. Hill b 9-27-1844 d 10-12-1930

Robert Emmett Hill b 1-14-1839 d 3-13-1918

Margaret Wier Lythgoe b 2-20-1832 d 6-26-1913

George Berkenhead Lythgoe b 8-29-1857 d 5-5-1930

Harriet Henry Lythgoe w E. G. Graydon b 1-22-1859
d 3-25-1878 m 2-28-1878

LONG CANES CEMETERY

Hannah Lythgoe d 6-3-1855 Aged 1 Year 3 Mon 11 Days

John Wier Lythgoe d 3-21-1874 Aged 1 Year 10 Mon 21 Days

Julia Kathlien dau Wm. N. & Mary E. Martin d 10-13-1848
  Aged 2 Years 10 Mon 17 Days

Wm. McIlwain b 1792 d 1882

Sarah Neil w Wm. McIlwain b 1807 d 1881

Nancy McIlwain b 1836 d 1915

Jane McIlwain b 1832 d 1849

Samuel McIlwain b 4-3-1849 d 11-27-1849

Elizabeth Neil d 1858

Eliza McIlwain b 1829 d 1849

E. N.

S. Mc.

J. Mc.

E. Mc.

William G. Gordon b 6-16-1832 d 1-9-1877 Confederate Soldier

Mary Hawthorn w W. G. Gordon b 8-11-1839 d 1-27-1912

Infant son W. G. & M. E. Gordon b 7-31-1873 d 8-1-1874

Unmarked grave of adult is next to above.

T. S. Gordon d 10-6-1917 Aged 80 Years

Mary Jane Gordon d 1-8-1892 Aged 42 Years

Jane Bughanan w John Donnald Sr. b County Antrim, Ireland
  2-5-1814 d 6-16-1885

Mary Bughanan w William Gordon b County Antrim, Ireland
  2-17-1809 d 1884

William Gordon b County Antrim, Ireland d 8-21-1869 Aged 68 Years

Unmarked grave of old Soldier next to above.

Jane McIlwain b 2-17-1792 d 4-17-1862

John McIlwain b 11-18-1813 d 6-15-1853

LONG CANES CEMETERY

Mary McIlwain b 4-23-1830 d 2-6-1907

Deborah Armon McIlwain cons W. M. McIlwain b 5-31-1831
d 9-12-1848

Matthew Donaldson d 10-23-1809 Aged 69 Years

Jennet Donaldson w Matthew Donaldson d 10-23-1809 Aged 73 Years

Jane Hadden dau Matthew & Elizabeth Wilson & w Rev'd. Isaac
Hadden b 1-17-1798 d 8-18-1830 Aged 32 Years 8 Mon

Francis Lavinia Hadden dau Rev. Isaac & Jane Hadden b 10-18-1829
d 10-15-1831 Aged 2 Years (nearly). In fourteen months she als
droped her day and went to join her Ma.in endless day.

Hannah Kirkwood w Hugh Kirkwood b 9-22-1802 d 7-22-1827
in 25th Year

Unmarked graves of two Children next to above.

Julia Josephine Spierin dau Thomas Piercy & Elizabeth Shauklin
Spierin b 12-2-1831 d 10-25-1832

Mrs. Patrick Spierin b 3-17-1770 d 2-19-1835 Aged 64 Years
11 Mon 2 Days

Mr. P. S. 1835

T. L. S. D. 1778

Agnes McCree d 8-28-1814 Aged 73 Years

John Robinson d 8-12-1863 Aged 49 Years

Edward McIlwain b 12-22-1824 d 1-5-1843

Thomas McIlwain d 2-9-1837 Aged 50 Years

Jane Robinson w Samuel Robinson d 7-5-1877 Aged 96 Years

Samuel Robinson d 3-11-1855 Aged 73 Years

Edward Robinson b 5-25-1825 d 11-11-1853

Margaret J. Gordon d 7-1-1849 Aged 15 Years

Mrs. Margaret Buchanan d 6-21-1848 In 68th Year Member the
Methodist Episcopal Church about 40 Years.

John B. Gordon d 8-27-1862 Aged 32 Years

E. R. Gordon d 6-22-1868 Aged 21 Years

Rev. Wm. H. Barr, D.D. d 1-9-1843 in 65th Year Pastor of
Upper Long Cane Church 33 Years.

LONG CANES CEMETERY

Susan Rosa dau Wm. H. & Rebecca Barr b 5-30-1831 d 7-30-1832

Hugh Reid d 7-2-1829 in 83rd Year Ruling Elder Upper Long Cane
for more than 10 Years

Margaret Reid w Hugh Reid d 12-27-1818 in 64th Year

Two unmarked graves are near above.

John Magill d 10-1842 in 24th Year

John T. Magill s John Magill d 2-1850 in 7th Year

Andrew Robinson d 4-27-1855 Aged 31 Years

Catherine Zimmerman b 1848 d 1936

Tena Andrews b 1841 d 1880

Sarah Hartgrove Liddell b 9-10-1844 d 1-12-1851 Aged 6 Years
4 Mon 2 Days

Eliza Ann Liddell b 12-25-1846 d 6-28-1847 Aged 6 Mon 2 Days

John Liddell d 5-6-1846 Aged Between 70 & 80 Years

Eliza Ann Davis dau James & Sarah Liddell b 5-23-1807
d 12-31-1846

George Liddell d 7-26-1840 in 30th Year

Henrietta Miller b 7-15-1841 d 4-3-1903

Corrie Miller McClung b 12-5-1845 d 7-5-1881

Capt. Charles Alexander McClung b 10-24-1842 d 4-25-1897

Mary Yarbrough McClung b 12-26-1869 d 10-7-1870

Rufus Morgan McClung b 5-15-1870 d 6-9-1879

W. R.

James S. Wilson d 7-24-1849 in 48th Year By his side lies
little Richard.

Mrs. J. S. Wilson d 3-21-1881 Aged 67 Years 5 Mon 13 Days

Sarah Liddell cons James Liddell d 4-20-1848 in 72nd Year

James Liddell Esq. d 1-23-1824 in 40th Year

John Miller b 1748 d 11-18-1811 in 63rd Year Native of
Pennsylvania who emigrated to S.C. 1770

Rachiel Miller w John Miller b 7-19-1765 d 10-19-1836
Aged 71 Years 3 Mon

William Miller s John & Rachiel Miller b 10-19-1797
d 8-27-1832

H. T. Miller b 5-21-1818 d 8-12-1857

E. C. Miller cons H. T. Miller b 8-13-1830 d 4-6-1852

Orrin Bowman s H. T. & E. C. Miller b 11-3-1855 d 4-8-1858

Elizabeth Hamilton dau H. T. & E. C. Miller b 1-21-1858
d 7-6-1858

John Watt

Samuel Watt b 1711 d 11-25-1802 Aged 61 Years Native of
Ireland. Landed at Charleston 10-18-1788.

Janet Watt cons Samuel Watt b 5-2-1753 d 2-3-1805

Mary Caroline Wardlaw b 8-6-1809 d 9-8-1813 A member of
this Church.

James H. Wardlaw d 3-30-1807 Being 4 Years 8 Mon 16 Days

Elizabeth A. Wardlaw dau James Wardlaw d 10-11-1804 Aged
7 Years 3 Mon 4 Days

A. Quay 11-9-1797

Tellula Elizabeth dau J. F. & Susan G. Griffin of Savannah,
Ga. d 6-26-1841 at Village of Abbeville, SC Aged 11 Mon
13 Days

James Frances Wardlaw s D. L. & S. R. Wardlaw b 2-5-1829
11-18-1834

Amanda E. dau Tho. C. & Jane E. Perrin b 11-9-1830 d 9-13-1831

Mary Elizabeth Wardlaw dau D. L. & Sarah R. Wardlaw b 3-21-1826
7-12-1827

Ann A. Louisa Wardlaw dau James & Hannah Wardlaw b 2-22-1819
d 10-12-1821

Hannah Wardlaw w James Wardlaw b 6-28-1778 d 11-14-1825
9 Children.

James Wardlaw b 12-6-1767 d 4-12-1842 Nearly 40 years Clerk
of Court for this District. From youth a member of this
Church.

Hugh Morah, Esq. d 2-4-1837 Aged 72 Years 5 Mon 26 Days

LONG CANES CEMETERY

James Gilmer, Sen. d 1-5-1796 Aged 67 Years

James Gilmer Jun. d 10-9-1819 Aged 61 Years 3 Mon

Unmarked grave of child next to above.

Zenot Gilmer Aged 7 Years

Ann Jen Gilmer

Five unmarked graves next to above.

Samuel s Robt. Gilmer d 7-28-1805 Aged 1 Year 10 Mon

John Gilmer s James Gilmer d 1-8-1810 Aged 17 Years 10 Mon

Crisalla Gilmer d 6-1-1816 Aged 9 Mon

Unmarked graves two adults next to above.

Robert Gilmer b 10-22-1794 d 11-14-1831

Matilda Gilmer b 8-23-1809 d 9-4-1859 Aged 50 Years

Susan A. Gilmer w John Gilmer b 1-26-1851 d 7-5-1906

Annie Gilmer b 11-23-1878 d 7-14-1880

Ida Gilmer b 9-5-1880 d 10-9-1885

Infant son John & Susan Gilmer 2-4-1887

John Gilmer b 12-19-1849 d 11-16-1892

James L. Sitton b 10-7-1849 d 11-7-1850

Clarance Edwin Sitton b 12-2-1847 d 12-5-1850

Harriet D. Sitton b 11-17-1855 d 5-31-1856

Sarah M. Benson dau Richard & Eliza A. Davis w James M.
  Benson b 1-31-1824 d 7-24-1856

Mrs. Isabella Miller b 2-24-1794 d 9-26-1865

Allen T. Miller b 1-22-1795 d 7-14-1856 Aged 61 Years
  5 Mon 22 Days

Eliza Ann dau A. T. & Isabella Miller b 1-29-1828 d 4-22-1835

Mary Anna dau A. T. & Isabella Miller b 8-9-1834 d 5-9-1835

William Twining s A. T. & Isabella Miller b 6-9-1837
  d 8-18-1839

S. P.

Unmarked grave is near above.

Nancy McFare

Unmarked graves three infants near above.

L. D. Bowie Confederate Soldier

Infant dau A. T. & J. B. McIlwain

Mary A. Darragh w John Darragh b 1828 d 3-27-1866

John Darragh b 3-1817 d 6-12-1901

J. A. Darragh b 12-10-1857 d 3-19-1876

Emily Haygood w W. W. Haygood dau John Darragh & her
    child b 7-10-1861 d 12-17-1890 m 6-11-1885

Unmarked grave of infant near above.

Clarience Edwin s Susan A. & Leroy J. Wilson d 5-1-1866
    Aged 4 Years 5 Mon 28 Days.

Anna dau Susan A. & Leroy J. Wilson d 12-15-1865
    Aged 2 Weeks 2 Days

Susan A. Wilson w Leroy J. Wilson dau Thomas & Mary
    Robertson b 7-18-1836 d 4-11-1873

Sarah U. Wilson w Leroy J. Wilson b 3-25-1848 d 12-15-1815

Leroy J. Wilson b 7-17-1836 d 8-9-1892

Lutesha M. dau Abram & Clarinda J. Gordon b 12-19-1855
    d 2-19-1861

Sarahe dau Abram & Clarinda J. Gordon b 10-4-1860 d 11-3-1860

Grace Wilson b 6-21-1907 d 1-15-1930 Woodmen of World Circle

Sarah Elizabeth Wilson w George T. Wilson b 12-31-1866
    d 6-29-1921

George T. Wilson b 7-2-1862 d 8-28-1929

Susie May dau G. T. & Lizzie Wilson b 12-18-1910 d 8-28-1911

Lola Earl b 12-5-1905 d 1-6-1906

Ola Pearl b 12-5-1905 d 3-7-1907

Eliza A. Stevenson b 9-28-1835 d 2-8-1870

LONG CANES CEMETERY

William Stevenson b 6-21-1837 d 5-23-1858

Thomas Stevenson b 6-7-1812 d 11-21-1879

Mary A. Stevenson b 11-7-1810 d 2-19-1890

Nancy Stevenson b 6-25-1850 d 8-19-1910

Unmarked adult grave near above.

Mrs. Mary Hill d 4-25-1856 Aged 70 Years Native of Ireland
and born near Ballynure, County Antrim.

Elizabeth Irwin d 7-25-1859 Aged 79 Years Native of County
Antrim, Ireland.

Robert W. Karey d 12-14-1848 in 40th Year Member Baptist
Church

Susan Stevenson w James C. Stevenson d 5-4-1891 Aged 61 Years

J. C. Stevenson b 12-15-1816 d 1-23-1886

Margaret Howlet d 9-5-1840 Aged 63 Years

Unmarked grave near above.

Hannah Armstrong dau W. G. & N. McWilliams b 5-8-1848
d 6-14-1855

David M. McWilliams s W. G. & Nancy McWilliams d 10-29-1862
Aged 11 Years 8 Mon 4 Days

Rebecca Stevenson w J. C. Stevenson dau W. & H. McCombs
b 9-25-1816 d 5-31-1847 Member Presbyterian Church

Infant son W. G. & Nancy McWilliams d 4-24-1847

Infant son W. G. & Nancy McWilliams d 6-25-1846

William McCombs d 3-11-1837 in 16th Year

Hannah McCombs cons William McCombs d 5-31-1864 Aged 79 Years

Mariah McComb d 10-4-1867 in 48th Year Father & Mother
lie by her side.

John McClellan b 4-19-1792 d 5-28-1863

Charles Dendy Allen b 3-25-1855 d 9-21-1902

James Albert Allen b 2-17-1868 d 3-13-1900

James A. Allen b 7-14-1825 d 3-4-1868

John Allen s J. A. & F. E. Allen b 3-9-1854 d 5-24-1854

Tommy Dendy s J. A. & F. E. Allen b 5-26-1852 d 4-23-1854
  Aged 1 Year 10 Mon

Dr. Thomas B. Dendy s Charles & Jenny Dendy b 7-11-1817
  d 12-23-1851

Infant dau & son J. T. & S. E. Owen 11-1-1865

Elise Apsly Dendy w Charles Dendy b 12-14-1803 d 2-4-1893
  m 5-1829

Charles Dendy b 3-20-1791 d 8-15-1859

Jennie Dendy w Charles Dendy b 4-5-1796 d 11-10-1826

Sarah Elenor Dendy b 8-3-1825 d 10-4-1826

Mary Jane Dendy b 3-7-1821 d 10-27-1826

Mrs. Mary Ellis Clemans M Charles Dendy d 2-19-1832 Aged 62

Harriet Dendy b 4-30-1819 d 8-25-1834

James Neyin Dendy b 6-7-1825 d 8-1835

Charles Newton Dendy b 5-2-1835 d 9-16-1839

John McClellan Dendy b 10-17-1841 d 5-13-1848

William Henry Dendy b 5-18-1832 d 1-26-1852

Jas Evans S.C. Mil. Rev. War

Ezekiel Evans 5 S.C. Regt. Cont'l. Army

Rebecca Gordon d 2-22-1854 in 77th Year

Robert Campbell Gordon d 1-21-1852 in 80th Year

Alax.r s John Willson d 2-12-1816 in 17th Year

Robert W. Willson d 3-1830 in 30th Year

Elizabeth Wilson w John Wilson d 1-9-1840

John Willson Sen. d 12-3-1845 Aged 73 Years

John Willson Jr. d 7-8-1844 in 36th Year

Maria Vashti Gordon b 9-8-1816 d 7-9-1837

Unmarked graves of two adults near above.

Margaret Gaines d 8-30-1857 Aged abt 58 Years

William Megill d 10-13-1838 in 76th Year A native of
   Ireland, emigrated to this Country 1788.

Agness Megill w Wm. Megill d 2-28-1831 in 78th Year
   Of reputable family in N.C. Member Prebyterian Church

Unmarked grave is near above.

J. Henry d 7-15-1797

Frances Henry d 1842 abt 67 Years Native of Ireland

W. S. 3-2-1801

Margaret Ann dau Peter & Rebecca Henry b 12-13-1853
   d 10-12-1860

May dau T. P. & M. T. Quarles b 10-24-1877

Mary T. Quarles w T. P. Quarles b 8-4-1840 d 11-9-1911

Thomas Perrin Quarles b 11-17-1841 d 11-24-1924
   Confederate Veteran

Thomas P. Thomson b 1-25-1857 d 8-13-1924

Frances Bradley w Thomas P. Thomson b 10-15-1857 d 2-12-1927

Janie Thomson w James Andrew Bowie b 5-5-1846 d 7-10-1922

James Andrew Bowie b 4-13-1845 d 6-16-1910

Margaret Martha Thomson w Thomas Thomson b 3-12-1825
   d 11-8-1885

Thomas Thomson b Tarbolton, Scotland 6-5-1813 d Abbeville, S.C.
   5-5-1881 Admitted to Bar 1837, elected Legislature 1846
   served until 1860. Colonel in Confederate Army, member of
   Senate 1862 till reconstruction, Judge from 1878 till death,
   Elder Presbyterian Church from 1871, Pres. Abbeville Bible
   Society from 1878.

Ninian Thomson s Thos. & Eliza Thomson b 4-13-1852 d 9-14-1865

Eliza Thomson b 11-20-1822 d 4-18-1862

Infant dau Thomas & Eliza Thomson

Ninian s Thomas & Eliza Thomson b 5-4-1847 d 5-3-1849

William s Peter & Rebecca Henry b 1-28-1850 d 7-2-1850

Unmarked grave of adult is near above.

Thomas Mc. Greer d 9-14-1795 Aged 63 Years

Mary Henry d 9-6-1860 abt 83 Years

Peter Henry d 10-28-1880 Aged abt 62 Years Confederate Soldier

Rebecca Henry d 4-10-1886 Aged .63 Years

2nd Lt. Dionysius A. Wilson Co A 2 SC Rifles CSA

Susan Ann dau F. A. & S. A. Wilson b 2-23-1855 d 8-4-1863

Macklin P. Wilson Co B 4 SC Regt CSA

John Claridge s I. B. & L. A. Courtright b 10-4-1850
    d 2-3-1855

James Fisher eldest s J. T. & E. W. Moore b 3-22-1848
    d 10-10-1859

John Allen d 7-6-1838 in 49th Year

Mrs. Jane L. Allen w John Allen b 9-26-1799 d 12-11-1864

James Clark Allen Co B Orr's S.C. Regt CSA

Clara Amanda dau John F. & Sarah A. Livingston b 10-20-1839
    d 8-16-1841

Margaret A. Livingston w Jno F. Livingston d 7-15-1853

Sarah A. Livingston cons John F. Livingston b 7-5-1809
    d 3-30-1843 Member Presbyterian Church

Doctor John Frazier Livingston b 12-2-1803 d 10-29-1867
    Presbyterian Elder 35 Years

Donald H. s Jno. F. & Sarah A. Livingston b 1-7-1828
    d 10-9-1843

William Donald s J. Fraser & M. F. Livingston b 1-5-1859
    d 2-21-1860

Julia McCaw dau J. F. & M. F. Livingston b 7-21-1866
    d 6-9-1874

Unmarked grave of child next to above.

1st Lieut. J. F. Livingston Co G J.S.C. Cav CSA

Mary McCaw b 9-24-1844 d 4-12-1932

Julia C. McCaw b 1833 d 1895

LONG CANES CEMETERY

Jane dau Charles H. & Catherine L. Allen b 10-10-1852
d 5-5-1855

Unmarked infant grave near above

Mary Toland d 7-20-1816

Mary Livingston w Henry Livingston, desc. d 12-2-1856
in 80th Year

Henry Livingston d 6-12-1836 in 75th Year

John E. Allen b 2-25-1824 d 7-12-1854

Louisa Jane Allen Smith b 9-20-1834 d 5-8-1855

Unmarked adult grave near above.

W. J. Smith s W. J. & I. Smith b 6-20-1865

Infant s W. J. & I. Smith b & d 7-6-1866

Belle dau W. J. & I. Smith b 5-14-1876 d 9-10-1876

Ione Smith w W. Joel Smith b 7-23-1837 d 11-3-1879

W. Joel Smith b 10-26-1833 d 10-20-1908 Confederate Soldier

Sarah L. Smith w W. Joel Smith b 2-17-1835 d 4-8-1904

Thomas Perrin Cothran b 10-24-1857 d 4-11-1934 Justice
Supreme Court

Ione Cothran w T. P. Cothran dau W. Joel & Ione Smith
b 11-7-1861 d 7-29-1887 m 1-6-1886

Mabel C. Upchurch w A. M. Smith b 11-16-1867 d 12-21-1894

Mamie Lou Smith b 8-26-1857 d 1-21-1917

Rosey Ann Gilmer eldest dau Sam. I. Watt w Andrew Bowie
& w Robert Gilmer d 9-22-1855 in 75th Year Member of
Presbyterian Church

Eliza A. Bowie w Langdon Bowie & eldest dau Rev. D. R. Coffin
of Tennessee d 10-6-1834 in 25th Year

Andrew Bowie d 1-26-1808 in 35th Year Member Presbyterian
Church

Rose Bowie w Major John Bowie d 3-29-1807 in 64th Year

Major John Bowie d 9-20-1827 in 88th Year Native of Dumbar-
tonshire, Scot. from where he emigrated to S.C. before the
Rev. War, Officer in Rev. War, member Presbyterian Church.

Susan Ann dau Langdon & Eliza A. Bowie b 2-16-1832
d 7-22-1832

Charles Coffin s Langdon & Eliza A. Bowie b 5-4-1830
d 5-4-1831

Alexander Samuel s John & Jane E. Bowie b 12-2-1831
d 10-26-1832 Aged 10 Mon 24 Days

Andrew Bowie Wardlaw b 11-5-1831 d 12-14-1888

Sally E. Wardlaw w A. B. Wardlaw b 12-30-1837 d 2-13-1885

Marnie c A. B. & S. E. Wardlaw b 3-12-1876 d 11-29-1878

Charles C. Wardlaw b 11-23-1848 d 8-4-1885 Confederate Soldier

Eliza Bowie w Robert H. Wardlaw b 6-8-1808 d 8-9-1883

Robert H. Wardlaw b 4-28-1807 d 7-18-1887

Clara A. dau James A. & Eliza L. Wardlaw b 12-8-1857
d 9-19-1858

Mary dau Jas. A. & Eliza L. Wardlaw b 12-29-1861 d 1-25-1862

James Alfred Wardlaw b 7-27-1833 d 9-29-1862

T. Perrin Wardlaw b Abbeville, S.C. 7-20-1847 d Augusta, Ga.
11-28-1815

Charles Coffin s Jas. S. & Susan W. Bowie b 5-27-1835
d 6-27-1835

Robert Henry Wardlaw b 11-6-1840 d 5-5-1865 Private Co B
Orr's SCV Last wound received near Petersburg Va. Died
at home.

Rosa c Robert H. & Eliza Wardlaw b 12-1-1834 d 9-9-1835

David A. s Robert H. & Eliza Wardlaw b Abbeville, S.C.
9-30-1846 d Memphis, Tenn. Yellow Fever 9-18-1878
Confederate Soldier

Lewis Joseph s Robert H. & Eliza Wardlaw b 6-3-1841 d 4-5-1845

Joseph Walter s Robert H. & Eliza Wardlaw b 2-14-1852
d 3-10-1853

Sarah Lydia dau James & M. M. Shillito b 11-6-1830 d 11-6-1832

Ada Moore dau Win C. & Eliza Moore Aged 8 Mon 13 Days

Infant c Win C. & Eliza Moore

30

LONG CANES CEMETERY

Sallie eldest dau Hiram W. & Fannie J. Lawson b 12-22-1847
    d 12-21-1855

Jennie youngest c James & M. M. Shillito Aged 11 Years
    8 Mon 16 Days

Lucy Wardlaw dau H. W. & F. J. Lawson b 5-29-1851 d 7-14-1862

Unmarked graves of adult & infant near above.

Hiram W. Lawson b Marlborough, N.Y. 7-22-1822 d 4-12-1881
    Confederate Soldier

Frances Jane Shillito w Hiram W. Lawson b 6-5-1829 d 5-8-1891

John Livingston Fair s Rev. R. A. & M. A. Fair b 10-4-1846
    d 2-16-1871

Annie dau Rev. R. A. & M. A. Fair b 5-16-1849 d 12-14-1867

William D. Wilson d 5-26-1935 Aged 74 Years 6 Mon 18 Days

William Alexander s Rev. R. A. & M. A. Fair b 12-14-1852
    d 5-9-1858

Eliza Thomson dau Rev. R. A. & M. A. Fair b 11-4-1852
    d 6-12-1858

Thomas Jefferson Fair s William & Elizabeth Fair of Newberry
    Dist. S.C. b 10-17-1806 d 1-25-1832 Graduated 12-1831
    South Carolina College

Jane Elizabeth dau Archibald & Eleanor Fair d 7-27-1828
    in 7th year

Eliza Jane Willson dau James & Anna Fair b 1-12-1817
    m John R. Willson 10-17-1833 d 8-11-1834

John R. Willson b 1-2-1807 d 9-12-1865

Unmarked adult grave near above.

Anna Eliza dau John R. & Mary Willson d 7-13-1848
    Aged 1 Year 4 Days

James Samuel s Capt. J. R. Willson b 9-5-1841 near Due West,
    Abbeville Dist. d 5-3-1863 Chancelersville, Va. of wounds
    Student Erskine College. Served Co B 17th SC Regt. 1861-
    1862 Co G Orr's Regt 1863. Member Presbyterian Church at
    Long Cane. Confederate Soldier.

Josephine Pamelia Fair d 10-24-1930 Aged 70 Years 4 Mon 21 Days

Katie Louise dau Rev. & Mrs. R. A. Fair b Abbeville, S.C.
    7-19-1863 d Newberry, S.C. 5-24-1881

Rev. J. Y. Fair, D.D. b 4-6-1851 d 6-30-1924 50 years in
  the ministry. Served Prebyterian Churches Canton, Miss.,
  Laurens, S.C. Charlotte, N.C., Richmond, Va., Savannah, Ga.

Rev. Robert Anderson Fair b Abbeville Co. S.C. 12-12-1820
  d Savannah, Ga. 4-11-1899 Graduated first class of Erskine
  College, practiced law 27 years Abbeville Bar, Lt. Col. 7th
  S.C. Regt.1861, ordained by S.C. Presbytery 1871, served
  Aveleigh Pres. Church Newberry, S.C. 12 years, Ruling Elder,
  Supt. Sunday School. Confederate Soldier.

Mary Amanda Allen w Rev. Robert A. Fair b Abbeville, S.C.
  2-27-1827 d Richmond, Va. 3-16-1867

Pascail Daus s P. D. & Emma E. Klugh b 12-16-1885 d 6-20-1886

Dollie dau G. W. & M. E. Syfan d 8-15-1882 Aged 4 Years 4 Mon

George Whitfield s G. W. & Mary Syfan d 6-26-1854 Aged 1 Year
  1 Day

Unmarked grave near above.Geo. W. Syfan b 5-22-1821 d 6-10-1901

Mary Eliza Syfan w G. W. Syfan Sr. d 1-14-1889 Aged 30 Years
  9 Mon 14 Days

Annie Ewart d 10-13-1883

A. R. Syfan b 7-14-1871 d 3-4-1915

Frances K. dau A. B. & K. H. Syfan b 3-12-1895 d 8-17-1896

Katie H. Syfan w A. R. Syfan b 7-22-1877 d 6-27-1896

E. M. Syfan b 4-21-1866 d 2-19-1912

William A. Lesly Co G 5 SC Reserves CSA Confederate Soldier

Robert L. Lesly

Augustus s Wm. & Martha Lesly b 7-26-1830 d 9-30-1832

Liuwellin L. s Wm. & Martha Lesly b 1-9-1836 d 7-29-1836

Martha E. Lesly cons Wm. Lesly b 6-4-1811 d 7-7-1842
  Member Presbyterian Church

Wm. Lesly b 4-25-1793 d 2-9-1867

Wm. E. s Wm. & Martha Lesly b 1-6-1836

Unmarked graves of adult & child near above.

Thomas Lesly b 10-7-1828 d 2-24-1862

LONG CANES CEMETERY

Eliza M. Lesly w James L. Lesly b 2-8-1837

Unmarked grave of adult near above.

Cornelia R. Lesly

Robert Hall Lesly

Elizabeth Lesly

John G. Frazer d 8-24-1840 in 43rd Year Stone erected by
    his aged Mother.

Unmarked grave near above.

Matthew Wilson & his wife Elizabeth Wilson

Infant s L. E. & A. Owen d 4-28-1841

Mary McCaslin dau T.E. & A. Owen d 1-12-1823

Lesly Harris Taggart s Moses & Mary Taggart d 9-20-1808
    Aged 8 Mon

Moses Jr. s Moses & Mary Taggart d 10-30-1822 in 26th Year

Mary Taggart w Moses Taggart Senr. d 7-21 in 63rd Year

Moses Taggart Sr.

John McCraven b 4-21-1792 d 10-11-1828

Nancy Eliza Kyle b 6-25-1811 d 8-23-1891

Jane A. Kyle b 4-22-1805 d 7-8-1837

James Kyle d 11-1814 Aged 40 Years

Aylett Chalmers w J. S. Cochran d 8-3-1899 Aged 34 Years

James D. Chalmers d 5-30-1894 Aged 60 Years Confederate Soldier

Christina Ramey w James D. Chalmers d 6-8-1912 Aged 78 Years

Celia Chalmers w T. A. White d 12-2-1889 Aged 21 Years

David Lesly b 6-1797 d 2-1854 Elder Presbyterian Church 22 years

Mrs. Louisa Lesly w David Lesly Aged 65 Years

Isaac Beckwith b 9-8-1786 Farmington Conn. d 8-29-1814

Alex. Chalmers d 8-2-1877 Aged 20 Years

Richard s J. D. & C. Chalmers Aged 18 Mon

Cecilia Fowler w Jas. W. Fowler dau Dr. A. W. & Mrs. Frances
 Chalmers of Newberry, S.C. b 1-23-1842 d 12-26-1868

Infant daughter 4-13-1866

Infant daughter 12-19-1868

Julia Cecelia dau J. W. & Jessie Trowbridge

Anna Branch dau J. W. & Jessie Trowbridge d 8-24-1877
 Aged 15 Mon

Infant J. S. & A. Cochran b 2-4-1898

Mrs. Elizabeth Medley Cobb w Edmond Cobb b 10-18-1818
 d 2-19-1864

Edmond Cobb b 2-10-1817 d 10-3-1859

James Medley Cobb & his wife Elizabeth Clisby
 Confederate Soldier

Carl Warner s A. F. & V. F. Lipford b 1-25-1858 d 3-18-1859

William M. Hughey b 5-18-1819 d 11-6-1864

Mrs. E. I. Hughey d 11-4-1897 Aged 72 Years

Mrs. E. Buchanan d 12-24-1872 Aged 83 Years

Nancy Kyle w James Kyle b 8-14-1774 d 7-18-1811

Sarah Virginia dau W. H. & N. C. Kyle Aged 18 Mon 27 Days

James s W. H. & N. C. Kyle d 8-2-1834 Aged 5 Years 4 Mon
 16 Days

Jane Louisa dau W. H. & N. C. Kyle d 9-16-1834 Aged 6 Years
 7 Mon 13 Days

Dr. D. M. Bass s Rev. Henry & Mrs. A. M. Bass b 12-15-1825
 d 9-24-1852 Aged 26 Years 9 Mon 9 Days

Louis Davis s John A. & Elizabeth G. Hamilton d 10-18-1855
 Aged 6 Years 1 Mon 3 Days

Unmarked adult grave near above.

Robert Strain & his wife Mary Strain

A. R. 1818

Five unmarked graves near above.

Nancy Hamilton w William Hamilton d 2-2-1804 Aged 21 Years
 7 Mon

LONG CANES CEMETERY

Unmarked graves of adult & child near above.

Francis Douglass s Thomas & Fannie Coogler b 11-9-1875
  d 8-22-1877

Thomas W. Coogler b 4-12-1831 d 11-15-1877

Unmarked grave of adult near above

Frances s Samuel & Elizabeth Branch d 5-11-1829 Aged 2 Years
  2 Mon

Samuel Branch d 7-19-1840 Aged 43 Years

Edward M. s John E. & Elizabeth Navy b 12-4-1843 d 6-28-1845

Infant dau Dr. Isaac Branch 5-6-1839

Infant dau Dr. Isaac Branch 3-8-1838

Infant son Dr. Isaac Branch 1-18-1836

Infant son Dr. Isaac Branch 4-14-1831

Infant son Dr. Isaac Branch 9-23-1832

Infant dau Dr. Isaac Branch 2-15-1835

Infant dau H. H. & M. B. Hall 8-22-1833

Infant son D. R. & M. F. Sondley 11-2-1853

Virginia C. Sondley d 10-16-1859 Aged 18 Years

Lula H. Haddon w B. M. Haddon dau Dr. I. & F. Branch
  b 6-29-1842 d 7-8-1871

D. R. Sondley b 1-1-1827 d 7-15-1870

Mary Frances Sondley w D. R. Sondley b 7-15-1833 d 5-20-1872

Hattie Shand dau Rev. Thomas G. & Hattie S. Herbert
  Aged 8 Years 10 Mon

Benjamin Gause s Rev. H. H. & Mrs. M. T. Durant of the
  S.C. Conference d 3-22-1855 Aged 1 Year, wanting 2 days.

Mrs. Fanny Branch w Dr. Isaac Branch Aged 66 Years

Dr. Isaac Branch Aged 72 Years

Annie Branch w W. T. Branch b 4-1851 d 7-1890

William Tully Branch b 4-23-1845 d 11-6-1903 A Mason &
  Confederate Soldier

LONG CANES CEMETERY

Unmarked graves four adults near above.

Robert Richey b 1-22-1787 d 12-22-1846

Unmarked graves four adults near above

Luvinia Tennent b 1808 d 1823

Charles Tennent b 12-25-1800 d 12-25-1820

Martha Tennent b 10-31-1779 d 4-30-1844

William oldest s Rev. Wm. & Susanah V. Tennent d 5-29-1816
  Aged 46 Years

Martha J. Lomax dau Wm. & Eliza Lomax d 10-5-1819 Aged 5 Mon

Eliza Lomax dau Wm. & Martha Tennent late cons Wm. Lomax
  d 9-12-1820 Aged 22 Years

William Lomax Esq. b 2-10-1782 d 6-6-1834 In 53rd Year

Unmarked grave of child near above.

B. C. S.

Deen

Unmarked grave adult near above.

T. H. C.

G. F. C.

Unmarked graves two adults near above.

D. W. N.

N. N.

M. C.

Unmarked grave near above.

Emma dau Eli & Mary A. Holliday b 8-9-1838 d 11-6-1839
  Aged 1 Year 2 Mon 27 Days

Unmarked grave Confederate Soldier near above.

Infant son Eli & Mary A. Holliday 5-5-1837

Richard D. Davis b 10-9-1802 d 5-25-1855

Garah Davis Esq. b Marland 11-9-1776 d 10-2-1822

LONG CANES CEMETERY

Mrs. Susan H. McBryde w John McBryde d 6-15-1843 Aged 26 Years

John McBryde b 1804 d 8-12-1865

Adam s John & Susan McBryde d 11-7-1840 Aged 11 Mon 17 Days

Andrew s John & Susan McBryde d 9-6-1839 Aged 1 Year

Robert McLaren Native of Scotland d 9-20-1835 in 53rd Year
Left a Brother

Adam McLaren Native of Scotland d 8-2-1826 in 50 Year
Leaving 8 children

Mrs. Agness McLaren cons Adam McLaren Native of Sterlingshire,
Scotland d 1-12-1851 Aged 74 Years   Leaving 2 sons and
5 daughters

John McLaren Sen. Native of Sterlingshire, Scotland d 9-17-1839
in 60th Year

Francis Henderson Jr. d 4-1850 in 51st Year

Thomas W. Baker s Capt. D.D. Baker, U.S. Marine Corps.
d 6-20-1852 Aged 16 Years 8 Mon

John McLaren Jr. b 11-20-1808 d 4-28-1864

A. A. Williams b 12-10-1827 d 8-27-1866

Jeremiah Shehan   Native County Limerick, Ireland d 4-30-1859
Aged 30 Years

Janet Hutton McLaren b 11-1798 d 10-1882

Agness Sarah Posey w B. V. Posey d 6-3-1849 Aged 19 Years
8 Mon

Martha A. Enright w John Enright d 8-28-1859 Aged 34 Years
10 Mon 4 Days

John Enright d 1-14-1873 Aged 64 Years

Thomas Geddings Enright bro. John Richard Enright b 3-11-1858
d 4-23-1883

John Richard Enright b 5-3-1855 d 4-4-1882

Unmarked grave near above.

A. Lythgoe s J. A. & S. M. Wier b 5-4-1862 d 6-3-1863

Alexr. Sloan s J. A. & S. M. Wier b 6-18-1857 d 1-22-1860

Susan Evaline dau J. A. & S. B. Wier b 8-28-1867 d 9-1-1870

LONG CANES CEMETERY

Leila May dau J. A. & S. B. Wier b 5-5-1870 d 9-22-1889

John Alex. Wier b 1-12-1816 d 9-8-1886 Confederate Soldier

Susan Benson w John A. Wier b 1-14-1832 d 2-24-1898

Kate dau Joel C. & Lillie P. Wier b 1-1-1886 d 11-9-1886

Ames H. Tusten b 7-26-1801 d 9-13-1854

Edna M. Tusten b 9-7-1803 d 3-23-1855

Argrove A. Tusten b 3-11-1841 d 8-11-1847 Aged 6 Years 11 Mon

James Thomas Tusten b 4-11-1834 d 9-13-1836 Aged 2 Years
   6 Mon 3 Days

Nathaniel Jefferson Davis b 12-9-1809 d 4-17-1874

Eliza C. Davis b 7-30-1803 d 4-9-1871

Arra T. Little d 7-26-1834 Aged 22 Years 9 Mon 15 Days

Jonnie s H. T. & A. A. Tusten d 9-12-1863 Aged 4 Years
   2 Mon 4 Days

Alice dau H. T. & A. A. Tusten d 9-25-1862 Aged 6 Years
   9 Mon 14 Days

J. H. Tusten s H. T. & A. A. Tusten b 3-22-1862 d 11-10-1877

Agnes Ann Tusten b 2-20-1838 d 9-28-1908

H. T. Tusten b 12-10-1828 d 2-7-1915 Confederate Soldier

Mrs. Nancy Holman b 10-9-1805 d 11-17-1826

Robert Word d 8-8-1830 in 50th Year

Harriet Idolia dau B. M. & E. V. Bleast b 8-18-1855
   d 8-14-1856

Three graves only have foot markers 1845 SER 1845

Ann Amelia b 12-28-1840 d 5-18-1851

"Little" Thornton b 7-24-1850 d 12-8-1851

Jane A. Marshall w Dr. J. W.W. Marshall & only dau Capt.
   Wm. & Frances J. Smith b 1-5-1828 d 5-21-1861 Aged
   33 Years 4 Mon 16 Days

Unmarked adult grave near above.

Mrs. Fannie C. Marshall d 1-2-1936 Aged 103 Years 9 Mon
   16 Days

Foster youngest c Dr. J. W. & Fannie J. Marshall
d 12-28-1879 Aged 5 Years 2 Mon 17 Days

Warren Waldo Marshall b 1872 d 1896

Mrs. Fannie J. Smith d 4-11-1877 Aged 70 Years 9 Days

Capt. William Smith d 9-11-1872 Aged 72 Years 3 Mon 20 Days

Nancy Crawford w Robert Crawford b Ireland 1801 d 4-9-1858
Aged near 57 Years

Robert Crawford b 12-1-1796 d 6-5-1878

Eugenia L. Crawford w R. W. Crawford b 8-25-1848 d 5-18-1880

Carrie E. dau R. W. & E. L. Crawford b 9-19-1879 d 6-7-1880

Martha E. Crawford w R. W. Crawford b 2-9-1855 d 6-7-1899

R. W. Crawford b 11-30-1832 d 10-11-1920 Confederate Soldier

Grace Crawford w W. Coke Baldwin b 8-4-1887 d 10-18-1917

Wesly C. Norwood, M.D. b 1806 d 1884 Erected by Members
S.C. Medical Assoc. 1917

Mrs. J. P. Norwood w Dr. W. C. Norwood d 4-5-1867 in 62nd Year

Louisa H.M. Patterson dau Dr. W. C. & J. P. Norwood b 2-18-1835
d 12-11-1857

W. R. Norwood d 5-24-1863 in 23rd Year Confederate Soldier

W. T. Norwood d 3-25-1865 in 27th Year Confederate Soldier

Sallie M. Norwood d 10-29-1869 in 23rd Year

Fannie N. Townsend dau Dr. W. C. Norwood d 5-29-1871 38 Years Old

Mrs. Corrie J. Brooks dau Capt. J. W. & S. A. Brooks
b 8-22-1857 d 4-27-1883

Elizabeth Brooks w J. W. Brooks dau N. & F. H. Moore
b 3-22-1818 d 2-27-1856 Member Presbyterian Church
16 years.

Moses Owen s M. D. & M. B. Roche d 9-1-1863 Aged 5 Years
3 Mon 13 Days

William L. McCracken b 12-9-1862 d 2-2-1866

J. W. Brooks b 2-26-1817 d 1-3-1895 Confederate Soldier

Sallie Brooks w J. W. Brooks b 7-7-1832 d 7-3-1892

LONG CANES CEMETERY

Paul s J. H. & L. M. Brooks b 7-11-1891 d 9-18-1894

Moses Taggart Owen b 10-31-1825 d 8-4-1863 from wound
received Boonsboro, Maryland 7-7-1863, m Martha Ann
Wideman 12-18-1855

Annie Owen b 6-13-1803 d 4-5-1870

Thomas E. Owen b 3-11-1802 d 5-11-1860

Martha Ann Wideman w Moses T. Owen b 12-26-1831 d 7-17-1875
Stone placed by a sister, Sarah Wideman Brown

A. T. Strain d 10-20-1856 in 40th Year

Elizabeth Ann Strain d 10-11-1839 in 25th Year

William s W. & N. J. Bowie b 7-24-1839 d 10-18-1841

Louisa A. Bowie 1852 "Just Seventeen"

William Bowie b 8-9-1782 d 3-12-1845

Sophia W. White w Lemuel Reid b 1-18-1824 d 11-23-1896

Lemuel Reid b 10-26-1818 d 5-11-1867   Confederate Soldier

James C. Reid b 7-14-1820 d 5-5-1864

Samuel Reid b 8-10-1788 d 7-24-1857

A. M. Reid b 8-2-1830 d 9-6-1855

Lizzie Reid dau L. & S. W. Reid b 10-19-1853 d 6-23-1854

Miss Sarah P. Barnett b 2-2-1828 d 1-29-1859

Susan Claudia Sproull w Charles Wm. Sproull dau John &
Mary Barnett & her Only Born d 10-7-1845 Aged 23 Years
3 Mon 7 Days

David T. s T. E. & A. Owen d 9-16-1846 Aged 5 Years
4 Mon 18 Days

Mary Anne dau Maurice D. & Bethia M. Roche d 9-28-1817
Aged 4 Mon 8 Days

Thomas E. s M.D. & B.M. Roche d 2-15-1850 Aged 1 Year
3 Mon 11 Days

Michael W. "The Interesting Son" William M. & Margaret
Mooney d 6-4-1854 Aged 3 Years 5 Mon 26 Days. Said
William & Margaret Mooney are natives of County
Waterford, Ireland.

John Jack Barnett b 11-12-1778 d 11-1-1868 Fourscore
   years & ten.

Nancy Akin dau Samuel & Mary Ann Marshall b County Tyrone,
   Ireland 6-19-1774 d 1-17-1843

Joseph Akin s William & Nancy Akin b 8-14-1798 d 12-13-1852

James Gray d 11-20-1855 abt 22 Years Native of County
   Antrim, Ireland.

Samuel Robinson d 1843 Aged 70 Years

Jane Robinson relict Samuel Robinson d 1852 Aged 70 Years

William Means d 3-14-1852 in 69th year

Mrs. Sallie Means w Wm. Means d 4-1-1867 in 67th Year

Sallie E. Means

John T. Lyon b 1827 d 1889

Joseph Lyon b 5-1-1787 d 3-16-1850

Elizabeth Cowan Lyon b 12-21-1791 d 7-9-1882

Samuel eldest s Joseph & Elizabeth Lyon b 11-28-1824
   d 2-7-1850

Frances Eugenia dau J. A. & Sarah J. Lyon b 9-1-1853
   d 6-23-1854

Joseph W. Lyon b 7-28-1829 d 10-9-1854

Unmarked adult grave near above.

Harvey T. s H. T. & H. B. Lyon b 2-10-1863 d 12-3-1867

Infant dau H. T. & H. B. Lyon 3-12-1861

Willie H. s H. T. & H. B. Lyon b 1-17-1859 d 5-8-1883

Dr. H. T. Lyon b 12-12-1830 d 5-29-1886

Harriet B. Dendy w Dr. H. T. Lyon b 10-2-1837 d 2-14-1922

Andrew Paslay b 3-30-1837 d 8-25-1862

Benjamin D. Barksdale b 10-14, 1827 d 2-10-1882

Elizabeth N. Richey w John B. Richey dau Wm. & Sarah
   McClinton b 2-24-1819 d 4-10-1850

Elmina Richey w John B. Richey dau Jerdon & Sarah Moseley
   b 5-23-1818 d 5-14-1848

LONG CANES CEMETERY

John H. Dusenbery d 7-27-1864 Aged 9 Years 6 Mon 10 Days

Unmarked graves three children near above.

George Dusenbery b 1-16-1819 d 8-11-1869

Wm. Langdon Bowie d 9-7-1851 in 24th Year

Samuel Bowie b 7-9-1788 d 1-6-1837 Left 5 children

Aletha Gilmer Aged 49 Years

Luana Winn w H. M. Winn b 3-23-1829 d 6-7-1861
  Aged 32 Years 3 Mon 14 Days

Henry M. Winn b 11-28-1815 d 3-27-1872 Aged 56 Years 4 Mon

Mary R. Winn w H. M. Winn b 7-16-1838 d 3-7-1889

Mrs. Leontina Kerr b 1-8-1824 d 11-23-1888

H. S. Kerr b 3-24-1824 d 2-10-1881 Confederate Soldier

Jane Cornelia Hughes w B. P. Hughes b 11-29-1810 d 6-2-1897

William P. Hughes b 4-7-1851 d 3-15-1867

Benjamin P. Hughes b 4-29-1811 d 4-27-1866

Johnny Dunn Only c B. P. & Jane C. Hughes b 11-30-1848
  d 7-30-1849 Aged 8 Mon

W. T. McDonald b 2-11-1846 d 7-12-1916 Confederate Soldier

Leila Anderson McDonald d 4-18-1929 Aged 65 Years 4 Mon 16 Days

Louisa R. Burn Vose b 3-24-1842 d 12-8-1923 m Batcheller
  Anderson & m Carsten Vose 12-7-1871

Carsten Vose b 1806 d 1884

Batcheller Anderson b 1823 d 12-1863

Unmarked adult grave near above.

Infant s Patrick A. & Lula C. Roche b 9-16-1901

Lula Cheatham w Patrick Roche b 1-9-1867 d 1-31-1918

Patrick A. Roche b 11-2-1855 d 3-29-1928

Sallie dau E. & S. A. Roche b 1872 d 1906

Katharine A. dau E. & S. A. Roche b 1866 d 1914

LONG CANES CEMETERY

Unmarked adult grave near above.

Edward Roche b 3-8-1819 d 6-13-1902

Sarah Shillito w Edward Roche b 1-25-1833 d 1-3-1902

Wm. E. Roche b 10-23-1864 Aged 5 Mon 16 Days

Margaret E. Roche d 4-10-1863 Aged 1 Year 5 Days

Mary A. Roche d 4-5-1863 Aged 2 Years 11 Mon 12 Days

Ann Rebecca Jackson d 2-29-1884 Aged 63 Years

Eliza Jackson w Thomas Jackson d 10-7-1839 in 39th Year

Thomas Jackson d 7-3-1884 Aged 86 Years

Matthew McDonald Esq. b 3-13-1820 d 6-12-1876

Mary Elizabeth Lomax w Lucien H. Lomax only dau Prof.
    David & Amanda Duncan b 4-30-1825 d 11-5-1851
    By her side a son James Lomax b 4-19-1849 d 10-29-1851

John Cunningham b 12-2-1782 d 2-10-1859

Frances Elizabeth Cunningham w Joel J. Cunningham
    b 9-2-1834 d 3-1-1855

Major Benjamin F. Cunningham b 4-14-1816 d 10-19-1853

Joel J. Cunningham b 1-23-1821 d 12-8-1874

Margaret V. Cunningham w Capt. Wm. R. Pool b 4-18-1823
    d 11-1-1899

Capt. John H. Sassard b Bordeaux, France d Abbeville
    2-9-1864 Aged 72 Years Member Methodist Church &
    St. Andrews Masonic Lodge, Charleston, SC

Clarence W. Davis grandson Capt. John H. Sassard
    b Charleston, SC d Abbeville 10-30-1862 Aged 10 Years

Unmarked adult grave near above.

Samuel W. Cochran Sr. b 9-22-1787 d 12-8-1863 Aged 76 Years
    2 Mon 17 Days

Unmarked adult grave near above.

H. O. Stevenson b 3-6-1849 d 12-9-1925

William Stevenson b 7-29-1814 d 9-18-1852

Jane Eleanor Crawford b 3-28-1816 d 6-26-1912

Margaret B. Magill w James Magill b 2-4-1818 d 7-12-1854

Infant dau James M. & Mary E. Perrin b 12-15-1850 d 12-5-1850

Thomas Chiles s James M. & Mary E. Perrin b 12-2-1851
   d 11-29-1852 Aged 11 Mon 27 Days

Mary Elizabeth Perrin w James M. Perrin b 11-2-1829
   d 8-8-1855

James M. Perrin b 6-8-1822 d Mortally wounded at Battle
   Chancelorsville, Va. 5-3-1863 died the following morn-
   ing. Graduated S.C. College, served Mexican War, Lawyer,
   Confederate Capt Jan. 1861. Fell mortally wounded in
   command of 1st Regt. Rifles SCV. Confederate Soldier.

Kittie C. Perrin w Col. James M. Perrin b 2-26-1832
   Fell asleep 9-7-1890

Joel S. Perrin b 10-31-1849 d 7-31-1875

Eunice C. Perrin b 1-21-1860 d 8-10-1885

William P. Keaton b 1-22-1830 d 9-18-1864

Edward F.M. Winn d 4-10-1854 Aged 25 Years 7 Mon 18 Days

Daniel F. Winn d 5-22-1843 Aged 26 Years 1 Mon 25 Days

Andrew Winn b 12-28-1785 d 3-28-1864 Aged 78 Years 3 Mon

Martha Winn w A. Winn b 7-19-1793 d 5-19-1865 Aged 71 Years
   10 Mon

Della Knox Douthart b 4-23-1859 d 6-1-1930

Mrs. Kate Strickler Beard d 5-27-1934 Aged 66 Years 8 Mon
   12 Days (Mortuary Marker)

John Knox b 8-31-1831 d 3-18-1887 Confederate Soldier

Mary C. Moore w John Knox b Town of Raloo County Antrim,
   Ireland d 7-2-1878 Aged 40 Years

Unmarked adult grave near above.

John infant s John & Della Knox 1887

Our Mother

Leila Thomson Quarles w S. Jenner Link b 10-17-1870 d 5-3-1897

Samuel Jenner Link b 2-18-1867 d 12-1-1921

Mrs. Grace Smith Link d 10-19-1936 Aged 59 Years

Infant sons S. J. & Leila T. Link 1894

Eliza Ann Giles Templeton b. 1848 d 1929

William Augustus Templeton b 1846 d 1914 Confederate Soldier

James Patterson Templeton b 1886 d 1901

John Archer Thomson b 4-26-1873 d 3-1-1893

John Allen Thomson b 4-5-1843 d 10-23-1878

Mrs. Lucy C. Thomson d 6-6-1933 Aged 89 Years 2 Mon 21 Days

R. A. Archer, M.D. b Pickensville 8-13-1818 d Abbeville
  10-1-1872

John H. Wilson b 10-8-1804 d 2-25-1869

Mrs. Sarah M. Templeton w Dr. W. T. Templeton d 4-1877
  Aged 52 Years

Dr. W. L. Templeton d 6-30-1881 Aged 67 Years

James Mabry Chiles Aged 22 Mon

Susan Emma Giles w James M. Giles b 7-6-1850 d 6-23-1889

Jas. M. Calvert d 3-27-1879 Aged 63 Years 3 Mon 5 Days
  Confederate Soldier

Lucinda Moore w Jas. M. Calvert b 11-15-1818 d 8-6-1883

James M. s D. C. & M. I. Calvert b 3-18-1883 d 6-16-1885

Lucy L. dau D. C. & M. Calvert b 7-9-1884 d 7-10-1885

Nancy D. dau D. C. & M. I. Calvert b 8-29-1887 d 6-1-1888

Annie Mary dau D. C. & M. I. Calvert b 1-29-1886 d 8-31-1890

D. C. Calvert b 3-27-1859 d 3-8-1899

Joseph T. Moore b 6-14-1825 d 11-12-1870

Unmarked graves two adults near above.

Sammie M. s Jas. H. & Mary Simmons b 10-26-1874 d 12-13-1877

Mary Simmons w Jas. H. Simmons dau J. T. & E. W. Moore
  b 2-26-1853 d 12-17-1880

Simmons

Lillie Etoile dau G. H. & L. J. Moore Aged 7 Mon 4 Days

LONG CANES CEMETERY

Unmarked adult grave near above.

J. T. Perry b 2-1-1853 d 6-10-1901

Unmarked adult grave near above.

Elizabeth McConnel b 11-15-1806 d 6-13-1886

Mary A.C. Winn w Robt. H. Winn b 3-7-1828 d 12-2-1888

R. H. Winn b 4-27-1814 d 2-14-1905   Confederate Soldier

Andrew W. s R. H. & M. A. Winn b 8-31-1866 d 11-16-1879

Parthena C. Winn b 6-2-1845 d 11-10-1857

Hiram Tilman s W. A. & Ivy Wardlaw b 2-3-1854 d 11-3-1908

William Alfred Wardlaw b 11-6-1816 d 10-10-1876

Ivy Wardlaw w W. A. Wardlaw b 11-15-1820 d 1-28-1863

Edward Tilman s W. A. & I. Wardlaw b 3-13-1841 d 6-8-1848

James Joseph s W. A. & I. Wardlaw b 9-23-1842 d 6-20-1843

Edward Robert s W. A. & I. Wardlaw b 4-15-1847 d 6-25-1854

William Alfred s W. A. & I. Wardlaw b 12-6-1851 d 3-30-1863

David Lewis Wardlaw b 1-21-1850 d 3-23-1914

James Witherspoon s Dr. J. J. & M.A. Wardlaw b 1-10-1840
d 7-6-1860 Member senior class S.C. College

Thornwell s Dr. Joseph J. & Mary Ann Wardlaw b 6-4-1842
d 7-13-1843 Aged 1 Year 1 Mon 9 Days

1st Sgt. Lewis Alfred Wardlaw s Dr. J. J. & M. A. Wardlaw
b Abbeville C.H., S.C. 1-4-1844 d at home 6-6-1863 of
wound at battle Chancellorsville, Va. Confederate Soldier

Dr. Joseph James Wardlaw s James & Hannah Wardlaw b Abbeville
C.H., S.C. 10-29-1814 d Walhalla, S.C. 7-3-1873

Mary Ann Wardlaw w Dr. J. J. Wardlaw dau Col. James H. &
Jane D. Witherspoon b Lancaster Co. S.C. 2-26-1818
d Columbia, S.C. 12-4-1890

James H.W. Sadler b 9-1835 d 12-1853 visiting relatives
in this District.

Harvey William Gordon b 5-17-1848 d 12-23-1925

Mary Jane McIlwain b 4-14-1847 d 11-23-1899

Honorable David Lewis Wardlaw b 3-28-1799 d 6-8-1873
Graduated S.C. College 1816, admitted to Bar 1820,
elected Legislature 1828, Speaker House Rep. 1836,
Judge Law Court 1841, Assoc. Justice Court Appeals
1865, Judge 27 years.

Mrs. Sarah R. Wardlaw w Hon. D. L. Wardlaw b 5-6-1807
d 6-17-1845

George Allen Wardlaw b 7-12-1837 d 7-9-1865 Graduated
S.C. College 1857, admitted to Bar 1859, entered
Confederate Army 1861, captured near Richmond, Va.
7-28-1864, Prisoner Fort Delaware, an only son &
brother.

Susan Caroline McGowan w Samuel McGowan dau David Lewis
Wardlaw b 4-3-1827 d 9-19-1878

Samuel McGowan b Laurens Co. 10-9-1819 d Abbeville 8-9-1897
Hero two wars, seven times wounded, Capt. Mexican War
1846-1848 U.S.A., Confederate War 1861-1865 Brig. Gen.
C.S.A., Member Legislature 1848-1860, elected Congress
1866, Assoc. Justice Supreme Court S.C. 1878-1894.

Susan Benet w William Christie Benet dau Samuel & Susan
McGowan b 7-6-1856 d 7-21-1898 m 5-3-1877 Leaves 4
sons.

William Christie Benet b 3-22-1846 d 8-17-1930 Native of
Scotland, Honor graduate Univ. Edinburgh, came to S.C.
1868, Teacher, Lawyer, Judge Circuit Courts S.C., m Susan
McGowan of Abbeville. Stone erected by four sons.

Ella Coulter Haskell b 3-3-1835 d 9-3-1887

Mary Sophia Haskell b 6-17-1859 d 6-21-1861

Samuel McGowan b 12-9-1854 d 8-1862

Sarah Wardlaw dau Samuel & Susan C. McGowan Aged 2 Years
2 Mon 18 Days

Lewis McGowan Aged 1 Year 10 Mon 4 Days

Alexander McGowan b 3-15-1864 d 8-1-1867

Samuel McG. Benet b 9-3-1878 d 6-7-1879

William McG. Benet d 7-2-1886 Aged 1 Year 12 Days

Thomas Samuel Perrin s Thomas & Jane E. Perrin b 3-10-1845
Fell in battle Chancellorsville, Va., Just past Eighteen.
Confederate Soldier.

William Henry Perrin s Thomas C. & Jane E. Perrin b 2-13-1838
Fell in battle at Gaines Mill, Richmond, Va. 6-27-1862.
Confederate Soldier

Francis Hugh s Thomas C. & Jane E. Perrin b 10-17-1846
d 9-13-1854

Robert C. s Thos. C. & Jane E. Perrin b 9-19-1852 d 12-29-1853

Hannah Clarke Perrin b 5-4-1836 d 12-6-1918

Thomas Chiles Perrin b 10-1-1805 d 5-14-1878 Graduated S.C.
College 1826, admitted to Bar 1828, married 1-19-1830,
elected Legislature 1842, Elected G & C.R.R. Co. 1853-1866
Joined Upper Long Cane under Dr. Turner 1844, Ruling Elder
18 years, Ruling Elder Presb. Church Abbeville til death.

Jane Eliza Perrin dau James & Hannah Wardlaw w Thomas C. Perrin
b 12-26-1811 d 9-9-1881

Lewis Wardlaw Perrin Jr. b 3-4-1875 d 8-31-1876

Mary McCaw Perrin b 11-5-1883 d 11-27-1886

Lewis Wardlaw Perrin b 5-21-1839 d 6-25-1907 Confederate Soldier

Mary Means Perrin b 9-19-1849 d 11-22-1934

Robert Walter s T. W. & E. H. Thomas b 9-13-1839 d 5-15-1854

Thomas Walter Thomas cons Elizabeth H. Thomas b St. Stephens
Parish, Charleston District, S.C. 3-9-1798 d 1-28-1855

Henry Walter s late T. W. & E. H. Thomas b 4-30-1844 Removed
from his sorrowing Mother 4-27-1855

Capt. Wm. Henry White b 11-23-1836 Killed on battlefield of
Second Manassas 8-30-1862 Confederate Soldier

Lucy White w John White b 4-21-1809 d 3-19-1890

John White b 12-3-1806 d 3-2-1882

Lucy Agnes dau John & Lucy White b 8-19-1841 d 6-24-1899

Nannie Amelia dau John & Lucy White w A. B. Wardlaw b 11-6-1845
d 11-9-1915

Mary J.E. dau R. C. & M. J. Starr b 10-3-1851 d 9-6-1853

Sarah E. Hughes w E. H. Hughes b 1-4-1869 d 6-25-1918

Unmarked infant grave near above.

Thomas s E. H. & S. E. Hughes b 8-29-1904 d 3-9-1905

LONG CANES CEMETERY

William H. s E. H. & S. E. Hughes b 5-21-1900 d 6-2-1902

Margaret Agness McMeen b 2-23-1813 d 10-3-1863 m John
   Shillito 12-24-1829 Aged 50 Years 7 Mon 26 Days

Unmarked adult grave near above.

Emma E. Link w E. T. Link b 10-24-1848 d 9-5-1910

Three unmarked graves near above.

Robert H. Cochran b 9-8-1835 d 4-13-1906 Confederate Soldier

Agnes Gilmer w R. H. Cochran b 2-22-1844 d 4-21-1918

Mary Sue dau R. H. & A. V. Cochran b 2-22-1886 d 11-11-1915

Caroline Etna dau R. H. & A. V. Cochran b 11-15-1888
   d 3-11-1920

Thomas Franklin Black d 1-26-1934 Aged 54 Years 4 Mon 20 Days
   (Mortuary Marker)

Eliza Ayer Bowie b 1836 d 1911

Willie Estelle Godbold w James S. Bowie Aged 27 Years

James Sheridan Bowie b 5-22-1875 d 8-22-1931

W. H. Long b 12-24-1850 d 9-15-1927

Ida Allen Long b 8-2-1849 d 12-9-1915

Edna Tusten w F. E. Harrison b 3-1-1871 d 2-25-1901

Dr. Francis E. Harrison b 2-9-1863 d 6-15-1931

Agnes dau F. E. & E. T. Harrison 1-20-1901

Fredrick W. Selleck b 7=8=1824 d 9-21-1853 Hero of Garita
   De Belen, By his Captain.

Joseph Togno A native of Ajaccio, Corsica d Suddenly
   2-5-1859 in 69th Year

Henry Crowell Thomas

Mary Louisa dau T. M. & Mary Ann Christian b 3-20-1856
   d 12-25-1858

Mary Ann Christian w T. M. Christian b 4-23-1833 d 3-22-1863

Thomas M. Christian d 3-7-1898 in 70th Year Masonic Emblem

Miss Arianah E. White in 20th Year

Miss Julia C. White in 18th Year

Celestea E. dau Frances & Matilda Sharp d 10-4-1852
   Aged 5 Years

William Walker Westfield b 7-15-1870 d 2-18-1931

Sarah J. Westfield b 1-14-1833 d 8-16-1911

Edward Westfield b 1-13-1825 d 10-18-1894 Confederate Soldier

John Livingston s Edward & Sarah L. Westfield b 3-24-1870
   Second Son Aged 6 Years

Virginia E. Westfield w Edward Westfield d 4-1-1856
   Aged 23 Years

Charley S. only son E. & V. E. Westfield d 7-30-1855
   Aged 2 Years 7 Mon

M. A. C.

Thomas Teal Confederate Soldier

R. L. Lester Confederate Soldier

Hardy Horn Confederate Soldier

John Garret Confederate Soldier

W. P. Duke Confederate Soldier

James Wardlaw Perrin b 5-8-1833 d 12-13-1890 Confederate Soldier

Mary J. Perrin w J. W. Perrin b 2-17-1835 d 1-29-1874

Lewis Clarke Clopton s J. W. & Mary J. Perrin b 1-28-1874
   d 5-15-1874

Jane Eliza dau J. W. & Mary J. Perrin b 12-1-1864 d 8-30-1870

Mary Campbell dau J. W. & Mary J. Perrin b 3-30-1866
   d 10-2-1867

Unmarked adult grave near above.

Jack s J. W. & Sarah A. Thomson b 5-23-1901 d 7-23-1905

Sarah Amanda Thomson w J. W. Thomson dau J. Wardlaw &
   Mary J. Perrin b 12-27-1861 d 7-1-1901 m 12-8-1885

Thomas s J. W. & Sarah A. Thomson b 2-16-1894 d 3-8-1895

Miss Anna Rosa Sassard b Charleston d Abbeville 12-2-1873
   Aged 28 Years

LONG CANES CEMETERY

Mrs. Henrietta Sassard d 11-9-1879 Aged 73 Years 1 Mon 16 Days

Joe E. Jones b 1869 d 1923

Ida G. Johnson Jones 1871

Mary Jones b 11-22-1831 d 6-20-1906

Robt. Jones b 10-18-1819 d 4-9-1878 Confederate Soldier

B. W. Jones b 1852 d 1904

T. F. Duncan, M.D. b Upson Co., Ga. 7-15-1831 d Abbeville
  1-13-1871

Lewis Perrin, M.D. b 5-6-1809 d 10-24-1880

Unmarked adult grave near above.

Uriah M. Mars d 1-4-1881 Aged 66 Years 9 Mon 28 Days

Lois Elizabeth Crawford w T. M. Miller b 6-10-1877 d 12-1-1927

Hugh Mack s J. T. & M. V. Miller d 11-12-1877 Aged 5 Years

Mary V. Miller b 4-1-1837 d 11-1-1895

John Miller b 11-15-1820 d 11-4-1898 Masonic Emblem

Thomas Virgil Miller b 2-23-1869 d 8-21-1934 Masonic Emblem

Sarah A. Newell b 8-20-1826 d 1-15-1899

Unmarked infant grave near above.

J. W. s D. E. & M. A. Newell b 9-30-1877 d 10-9-1878

L. W. s D. E. & M. A. Newell b 12-6-1883 d 5-3-1886

Unmarked adult grave near above.

Margaret A. Uldrick w D. E. Newell b 5-29-1854 d 2-6-1925

Unmarked adult grave near above.

Susan A. Wilson w J. W. Keller, M.D. d 2-23-1917

James Wesley Keller b 9-16-1833 d 9-12-1921

Mrs. L. R. Keller w Dr. J. W. Keller d 10-14-1879 Aged 38 Years

Willie Isaac s Dr. J. W. & L. R. Keller d 9-17-1880 Aged 3 Years

Mary S. dau Dr. J. W. & L. R. Keller b 2-4-1872 d 11-16-1892

LONG CANES CEMETERY

Jane G. Gillespie b 6-28-1805 d 9-1-1898 Member Upper Long Cane Church 70 Years.

Miss Mary M. Gillespie d 1-29-1880 in 77th Year Consistent member Upper Long Cane Church 47 Years.

Henry B. Gillespie b 1-15-1812 d 3-13-1885 Brother Confederate Soldier

Edwin Lindsay Wilson b 5-13-1878 d 3-14-1922

Mary Elizabeth Wilson w William Wilson b 2-2-1834 d 2-12-1900

William Wilson b 8-26-1821 d 9-20-1904

Mary Virginia Wilson b 7-16-1865 d 10-21-1921

Miss Emma H. Wilson d 2-5-1933 Aged 70 Years (Mortuary Marker)

Pearlie Parker dau E. H. McBride

Infants dau & s W. B. & M. J. Uldrick b 10-6-1887 d 11-17-1887

Son of W. B. & M. J. Uldrick b 2-7-1890 d 3-1890

S. M. Uldrick d 3-8-1886 Aged 21 Years 6 Mon 2 Days

J. J. Uldrick b 12-16-1855 d 2-4-1876

Mrs. Jane Y. Uldrick w J. E. Uldrick d 3-1-1893 Aged 58 Years & 3 Mon

J. E. Uldrick b 2-22-1830 d 5-10-1899

Joseph P. s J. E. & J. Y. Uldrick b 12-23-1866 d 9-29-1890

Lavinia McMillan w Thomas McMillan b 5-10-1802 d 6-10-1884

Unmarked grave two adults & infant near above.

T. W. McMillan b 10-23-1826 d 5-14-1892

Nancy Elizabeth McMillan w T. W. McMillan b 3-2-1835 d 6-25-1896

Infant s Wm. N & Ada Graydon

Unmarked adult grave near above.

Elizabeth Wharton w John A. Hamilton b 12-18-1810 d 7-17-1895

John A. Hamilton b 2-2-1807 d 11-7-1876

Unmarked graves thee adults near above.

Gustave E. Cox b 1-2-1871 d 2-27-1904

LONG CANES CEMETERY

Anne Eliza Hill w Charles A. Cox b 1836 d 1919

Charles Cox b 5-28-1828 d 4-29-1877 Confederate Soldier

Charles T. Jr. s Charles & Annie E. Cox b 1-15-1864
   d 11-2-1881

Mary Magill Means w James William Means b 4-7-1839 d 7-20-1875

Two Infant s T. A. & F. A. Sullivan b 1873 & 1874

Gussie dau E. M. & A. K. DuPre b 9-6-1886 d 8-9-1924

Mary P. DuPre w J.F.C. DuPre b 5-27-1833 d 3-15-1906

J.F.C. DuPre b 8-1-1831 d 8-25-1899 Confederate Soldier
   & Masonic Emblem

Anna Rosa dau J. F.C. DuPre b 1-27-1874 d 3-1-1875

Unmarked infant grave near above.

Annie Russell b 5-1-1837 d 9-10-1924

Sadie dau L. H. & M. A. Russell d 12-23-1874 Aged 3 Mon

Louis Henry Russell b 5-12-1836 d 4-19-1910 Lieut. Co A
   1st S.C. Cav CSA

Unmarked adult grave near above.

J. Hollinshead

Jerusha McCord d 6-23-1894 Aged 83 Years

Unmarked adult grave near above.

Mary Jane Gordon b 9-28-1838 d 8-30-1875 Aged 37 Years

Robert Campbell Gordon b 6-22-1865 d 8-14-1873

James Gordon b 5-19-1804 d 5-31-1872

Unmarked graves two adults near above.

Harvay A. Douglass b 11-15-1880 d 5-14-1905

Margaret E. Douglass w G. A. Douglass d 12-27-1912

G. A. Douglass b 10-30-1837 d 4-27-1904 Confederate Soldier

Lizzie G. Douglass w G. A. Douglass d 5-2-1883 Aged 40 Years
   2 Mon 29 Days

Infant dau G. A. & Lizzie Douglass 3-15-1883

LONG CANES CEMETERY

Infant s G. A. & Lizzie Douglass 7-10-1875

Infant s G. A. & Lizzie Douglass 12-16-1869

Infant dau G. A. & Lizzie Douglass 5-6-1864

Essie D. Douglass d 12-6-1902   Erected by George C.
Douglass, her brother.

Wade H. Douglass b 5-30-1876 d 10-14-1904

LeRoy C. Wilson d 7-23-1886 Aged 79 Years 2 Mon 8 Days.

R. Evelina Wilson w LeRoy C. Wilson d 3-12-1871
Aged 63 Years 2 Mon 5 Days

Joseph Locke Evans d 11-8-1924

Stella Douglass w James F. Hutto d 7-3-1907

Andrew J. Ferguson b 2-18-1832 d 6-17-1897

Susan A. Ferguson b 9-4-1832 d 12-5-1912

Unmarked graves three adults near above.

Chloe J. Barksdale w Benj. Barksdale b 8-14-1806 d 3-3-1885

Unmarked adult grave near above.

William T. McIlwain d 9-25-1871 Aged 29 Years 1 Mon 11 Days
Confederate Soldier

Unmarked adult & infant graves near above.

Dr. Thomas Lee d 10-6-1870 in 60th Year

Unmarked graves two adults near above.

Thomas C. Seal b 3-3-1838 d 10-30-1925 Confederate Soldier

Lavonia R. Seal b 4-4-1841 d 7-20-1926

Willie Seal Smith b 3-20-1883 d 2-28-1914

Willie May dau T. C. & Livonia L. Seal   9-8-1876
Aged 4 Mon 27 Days

Mary Livonia dau T. C. & Livonia L. d 5-18-1875
Aged 5 Years 2 Mon 13 Days

Rosa dau T. C. & Livonia L. Seal d 8-29-1872
Aged 1 Year 1 Mon 2 Days

Dessie dau J. D. & Dessie King b 9-7-1898 d 3-13-1889

LONG CANES CEMETERY

Jane C. King b 1-6-1832 d 4-29-1896

Martha Aveline Ellis b 6-14-1834 d 11-21-1893

Mary S. Newell d 2-17-1885 Aged 94 Years

Wm. T. Newell d 8-19-1875 Aged 80 Years

Fannie A. King w J. D. King b 5-29-1859 d 8-26-1895

Dessie Gillan w J. D. King b 8-26-1873 d 11-5-1898

Florence Annie dau J. D. & Dessie King b 7-6-1897 d 7-21-1898

G. Thomas s J. D. & F. A. King d 10-17-1881 Aged 1 Year
   2 Mon 28 Days

W. Sloan s J. D. & F. A. King d 12-18-1879 Aged 2 Years
   5 Mon 5 Days

Essie Jane dau J. D. & F. A. King b 9-30-1894 d 7-1896

C. V. Hammond b 10-1-1843 d 12-4-1912 Confederate Soldier

Mary Rutledge w C. V. Hammond b 7-10-1845 d 2-14-1909

Arthur S. s C. V. & Mary Hammond d 9-11-1886 Aged 14 Years

Twin boys s C. V. & M. P. Hammond b 12-4-1885
   Barney V. d 6-15-1886 & Frank D. d 6-24-1886

Infant dau C. V. & M. P. Hammond d 7-22-1882

Infant dau C. V. & M. P. Hammond d 3-12-1881

Fannie dau C. V. & M. P. Hammond d 8-19-1880 Aged 5 Mon 20 Days

Jimmie s C. V. & M. P. Hammond d 5-25-1870

Hannah Clarke Cothran w John C. Cothran b 12-1-1862 d 9-23-1913

Emma Chiles Cothran w James S. Cothran b Abbeville, S.C.
   11-5-1834 d Greenville, S.C. 9-21-1916

James Sproull Cothran b 8-8-1830 m 7-17-1856 to Emma C.
   Perrin d 12-5-1897 Practiced Law Abbeville 1854-1861,
   Confederate Soldier 1861-1865, Capt. Co. B Orr's Rifles,
   Resumed Law practice 1866, Solicitor 8th Circuit 1876-
   1881, Circuit Judge 1881-1886, Member Congress 1886-1891,
   Practiced Law Greenville 1891-1897, United with Presbyterian
   Church Upper Long Cane 12-28-1866, Ordained & installed Elder
   of Abbeville Pres. Church 4-26-1886, Elder 2nd Pres. Church
   Greenville, S.C. 2-2-1896. Confederate Soldier

Rebecca C. Cothran w J. Allen Smith b 4-8-1856 d 1-8-1883

Infant s J. A. & B. C. Smith 1883

Mary Elizabeth dau James S. & Emma C. Cothran b 12-1-1862
d 2-20-1864

James Sproull Jr. s James S. & Emma C. Cothran b 4-25-1865
d 11-5-1865

Jane Eliza dau James S. & Emma C. Cothran b 9-9-1861 d 11-5-1861

Dila W. Clark b 2-2-1805 d 3-16-1877

Unmarked graves two adults near above.

Mary E. Clark d 4-1-1918 Aged 64 Years 9 Mon 27 Days (Mortuary
Marker)

Unmarked adult & infant graves near above.

Infant s S. E. & M. C. Price b & d 7-9-1888

Infant dau S. E. & M. C. Price b & d 5-23-1889

Unmarked adult grave neat above.

S. E. Price b 7-18-1858 d 3-2-1931

Corrie Price w S. E. Price b 1-26-1868 d 9-30-1912

Hattie Black Price b 6-7-1855 d 1-8-1923

James L. Price b 7-16-1885 d 10-28-1910

Mary A. Price w B. F. Price b 6-27-1850 d 2-18-1888

B. F. Price b 12-7-1846 d 5-20-1928

E. Alice Millford w J. C. Wosmansky & w J. H. Simmons
b 8-18-1853 d 2-29-1904

John Charles Wosmansky b Austria 12-23-1847 d 8-2-1877

T. Baily Millford b 7-13-1817 d 12-9-1877

Sarah A. Millford w T. B. Millford d 5-28-1874 Aged 48 Years

Sallie A. Miller w Chas. A. McClung b 4-30-1843 d 5-7-1914

Henrietta Kerr b 12-17-1901 d 7-23-1902

Amos Davis Kerr b 2-15-1907 d 8-27-1908

John Davis Kerr b 1-6-1872 d 7-28-1931

J. Edward s J. E. & M. E. Jackson b 9-6-1889 d 3-13-1894

Unmarked graves two adults near above.

Capt. Jas. T. Liddell b 11-8-1813 d 11-10-1873

Mrs. Mollie L. Cunningham b 4-13-1843 d 10-14-1864

Louisa Ramsay Liddell b 9-4-1859 d 3-12-1862

Hattie Turner Liddell b 1-13-1863 d 6-16-1864

Thomas Cunningham Liddell b 5-12-1848 d 5-29-1856
    Aged 8 Years 17 Days

Unmarked graves two adults near above.

Wm. F. Perrin b 1870 d 1934

Unmarked graves two adults & infant near above.

Infant s A. C. & S. M. Elders d 10-30-1856 Aged 8 Days

Sarah Jane Eakin b 1-16-1848 d 5-21-1918

Lela A. Eakin b 8-8-1868 d 2-11-1915

Orson Rawley s G. E. & S. T. Tarrington b 1-30-1862
    d 5-26-1862

Essie dau T. W. & I. N. McCord b 9-19-1894 d 10-10-1894

Sarah Eakins b 11-7-1816 d 8-6-1882

Evaline E. Eakins w B. H. Eakins d 2-15-1882 Aged 49 Years
    Member Greenville Presbyterian Church

Essa Claton youngest dau B. H. & E. E. Eakins d 1-8-1874

Infant child, not named, dau B. H. & E. E. Eakin
    b 8-10-1861 Aged 3 Weeks

William H. Eakin b 9-5-1819 d 1-24-1850

Benjamin H. Eakin b 9-9-1820 d 8-3-1891

Rebecca J. Eakin cons Benjamin H. Eakin dau A. & M. Winn
    b 1-17-1822 d 7-28-1854

Sarah Eakin cons Joseph Eakin Sen. d 8-18-1847 in 72nd Year

Joseph Eakin Sen. d 4-29-1847 in 74th Year

Georgianna B. Eakin dau B. H. & E. E. Eakin b 11-7-1862
    d 12-3-1865

Unmarked adult grave near above.

LONG CANES CEMETERY

Ida K. dau W. E. & Ida R. Morrison b 1-5-1891 d 5-21-1896

Ida R. McKee w W. E. Morrison b 2-6-1854 d 12-1-1898

Infant c W. E. & I. R. Morrison

W. Clarence s W. E. & I. R. Morrison b 1-13-1880 d 1-11-1900

Miss Ann Eliza Morrison d 2-17-1937 Aged 48 Years (Mortuary
Marker)

William Samuel Wilson b 11-13-1856 d 8-1-1930 Masonic Emblem

Mary Josephine Wilson b 12-31-1856 d 5-17-1931

Herbert A. s W. S. & M. J. Wilson b 8-28-1895 d 6-11-1898

William J. s W. S. & M. J. Wilson b 2-5-1883 d 1-17-1891

Unmarked adult grave near above.

Isaac W. Dansby b 9-26-1829 d 12-12-1897 Confederate Soldier

Mary Anna Branson w Isaac W. Dansby b 10-31-1833 d 3-6-1911

Samuel R. Douglas b 2-23-1855 d 1-7-1901

Kitty Frances Dansby w S. R. Douglas & w F. M. Robertson
b 9-9-1865 d 2-28-1933

Frank M. Robertson b 8-18-1867 d 8-26-1910

Frank s E. B. & Eliza T. Gary d 10-14-1888 Aged 7 Years

Agnes dau E. B. & Eliza T. Gary d 11-1-1888 Aged 10 Years
3 Mon

Hiram Tusten s Eugene B. & Eliza T. Gary b 12-3-1896 d 2-15-1897

Ernest Gary b 12-3-1896 d 3-1-1914

Eugene B. Gary Jr. b 4-16-1890 d 10-14-1918 Died in France
World War Veteran

Frank F. Gary, M.D. b 11-4-1829 d 12-31-1887 Confederate Soldier

Mary Caroline Blackburn w Frank F. Gary b 8-26-1833
d 2-9-1918

Eugene Blackburn Gary b 8-22-1854 d 12-10-1926 Lieutenant
Governor 1890-1893, Assoc. Justice Supreme Court 1833-
1912, Chief Justice Supreme Court 1912-1926.

Sloan A. Hall b 1-24-1871 d 1-4-1927

LONG CANES CEMETERY

Frank Boyd Gary b 3-9-1860 d 12-7-1922 Speaker House of Representatives 1896-1900, United States Senator 1908-1909, Circuit Judge 1912-1922.

George Carroll Swetenburg h Mary J. Milford s B. F. & M. E. Swetenburg b 5-25-1896 d 10-10-1929 World War Veteran

Unmarked graves two infants near above.

T. E. Kinard b 1860 d 1905 Born Newberry, S.C.

Lola A. White w T. E. Kinard b 1869 d 1935 Born Forsythe Co. N.C.

Rev. J. H. White b 12-7-1829 d 9-11-1895

Eleanor Dean w Rev. J. H. White b 1844 d 1909 Born Forsythe Co. N.C.

Hiram Tusten s W. W. & M. T. Bradley b 1-9-1896 d 9-17-1896

A. M. McCord b 2-9-1880 d 1-20-1926

William L. McCord b 1829 d 1906 Confederate Soldier

Margaret Elizabeth Stevenson w William L. McCord b 4-8-1853 d 7-13-1930

Nellie dau W. L. & M. L. McCord Aged 1 Year 7 Mon

David Augustus Dewey b 12-9-1875 d 3-5-1918

Ida dau R. B. & E. J. Haddon b 1893 d 1914

Calvin s R. B. & E. J. Haddon b 3-13-1900 d 12-2-1901

R. B. Haddon b 8-15-1859 d 8-8-1900

Matthew C. Owen b County Antrim, Ireland 1822 Emigrated to America 1840 d 3-27-1892 Confederate Soldier

W. A. Stewart b 6-15-1830 d 8-14-1916 Confederate Soldier

Louessa Stewart Stone d 8-20-1921 Aged 53 Years 3 Mon 10 Days (Mortuary Marker)

Unmarked graves three adults near above.

Norma Elizabeth Brown d 3-13-1933 Aged 5 Days

Unmarked infant grave near above.

Joseph D. Wilson, M.D. b 2-15-1864 d 9-29-1919

Robert McGowan s Samuel Lane & Elizabeth Clark Hill b 8-24-1856 d 11-13-1929

Mary Chapin Moore w Robert McGowan Hill b 10-10-1858
d 1-25-1934

Bessie dau R. M. & M. C. Hill b 1883 d 1901

Mamie Lawson w Robt. S. Link b 9-11-1863 d 9-23-1901

Emily Mary Schuck Link d 1-20-1936 Aged 36 Years
(Mortuary Marker)

Unmarked grave World War Veteran American Legion U.S.

Unmarked graves two adults & child near above.

Willie C. Moore Morton b 3-4-1865 d 3-4-1931

James Payne Morton b 5-2-1902 d 10-26-1924

Augustus Fisher Morton b 7-27-1899 d 11-27-1920

John W. Sign Jr. b 1870 d 1908

Mary Shillito w Paul E. Anderson b 1883 d 1910

Unmarked infant grave near above.

William C. Moore b 8-11-1833 d 10-1-1909 Confederate Soldier

Ann Margaret Moore b 1-2-1868 d 7-18-1908

Elizabeth G. Moore b 3-18-1861 d 7-4-1899

Unmarked grave of child near above.

Elizabeth C. Shillito w William C. Moore b 4-24-1833
d 10-9-1886

Unmarked graves two children near above.

John W. Sign b 1839 d 1915 Confederate Soldier

Julia Shillito w J. W. Sign b 1843 d 1909

Lewis W. Sign b 1872 d 1895

Jimmie Elwell s J. W. & Julia Sign d 1870 Aged 2½ Years

Unmarked grave Confederate Soldier near above.

Unmarked graves seven adults & three infants near above.

Andrew W. Shillito b 1-11-1794 d 10-7-1869

Unmarked graves five adults near above.

LONG CANES CEMETERY

Samuel Goode Thomson D.D.S. b 5-18-1858 d 8-14-1929

Unmarked infant grave near above.

Mary Jane dau T. J. & L. A. Robinson b 9-2-1900 d 5-24-1915

Thomas J. Robinson b 7-3-1863 d 2-18-1914

Leila A. Robinson w T. J. Robinson b 7-9-1862 d 7-31-1906

John Andrew Newell d 5-27-1904 (Mortuary Marker)

John Henry Ashley b 4-3-1862 d 5-12-1906

Evalina Viola Eakin w John Henry Ashley b 7-27-1866
    d 3-13-1929

Robert Allen Hagen b 9-13-1895 d 8-11-1933

Pressly

John Ebenezer Pressly, M.D. b 9-29-1882 d 6-8-1932
    World War Veteran

Jacob Kurg d 1-30-1885 Aged 53 Years 1 Mon 17 Days
    Native Switzerland, emigrated to this country 1852
    Confederated Soldier

Unmarked graves two adults near above.

Mary Alice dau J. F. & E. E. Langley b 8-29-1904
    d 8-19-1905

Alice Eugenia Robison d 10-25-1931 Aged 75 Years 10 Mon
    13 Days (Mortuary Marker)

Andy B. Robison d 9-21-1929 Aged 74 Years 2 Mon 28 Days
    (Mortuary Marker)

J. J. Brunson b 1853 d 11-13-1914 Masonic Emblem

Clara Gay Cochran b 1875 d 1932

John R. Nickles b 7-19-1879 d 8-23-1933

Children of J. S. & Kate Hammond 1876 & 1877

Joseph Harold s W. S. & A. E. Hammond b 9-26-1903 d 1-10-1904

Unmarked graves two adults near above.

H. Scott Hammond b 6-4-1879 d 7-6-1924

Unmarked adult grave near above.

Willie Coogler w E. L. Wilson b 2-3-1865 d 8-12-1897

E. L. Wilson b 10-3-1857 d 11-23-1909

Infant s E. L. & W. C. Wilson

Infant s E. L. & W. C. Wilson

Margie Elizabeth w J. A. Reid dau J. T. & M. E. Baskin
   b 3-27-1847 d 5-26-1890

James A. Reid b 12-3-1845 d 8-8-1896 Woodmen of World
   Confederate Soldier

Lucia W. Reid w Rev. W. G. Ewart b 12-31-1870 Fell Asleep
   8-2-1900

Unmarked adult grave near above.

Walter Eugene Johnson b 8-21-1876 d 12-26-1931

Frances s W. E. & Lorena Johnson b 1-5-1923 d 4-7-1923

Fannie E. Means b 12-2-1838 d 6-10-1914

Mary L. Means b 9-26-1831 d 12-10-1920   Aunt Mamie

Fannie Eugenia dau A. G. & Lizzie Cochran d 7-13-1886
   Aged 4 Mon

Lillie Brooks w Richard C. Wilson b 11-14-1862 d 11-13-1926

Richard C. Wilson b 11-14-1862 d 4-3-1934

Sarah Abigail Wilson w Courtney A. Wilson b 1833 d 1922

Luis w John Dees Jr. dau R. C. & L. W. Wilson b 10-15-1889
   d 9-4-1916

Infant s R. C. & L. W. Wilson b & d 9-16-1885

Jeannette dau S. F. & F. E. Nance b 7-2-1896 d 2-4-1913

Samuel F. Nance b 1857 d 1919

Unmarked adult grave near above

William H. Morese b 7-19-1870 d 4-21-1908

Rev. A. A. Morse b 3-29-1819 d 6-17-1894 Confederate Soldier

Caroline Teague w Rev. Albert A. Morse b 8-20-1828 d 9-8-1901

Amos B. Morse d 11-29-1928 Aged 73 Years 8 Mon 21 Days
   (Mortuary Marker)

Janie Morse w Amos B. Morse b 6-6-1860 d 4-13-1902

Lucy dau A. B. & J. A. Morse Aged 5 Mon

Richard Sondley b 1891 d 1914

Child L. P. & Annie B. Sondley b 10-12-1923 d 5-28-1925

Infant L. T. & M. L. Uldrick b 1-24-1898 d 1-26-1898

Infant sons L. T. & Mamie L. Uldrick

Unmarked infant grave near above.

Mamie L. Uldrick w L. T. Uldrick b 8-19-1878 d 8-3-1899

Sarah Eliza White w George White dau Thomas Chiles & Jane
   Wardlaw Perrin b 1-1-1841 d 4-10-1925

George White s John & Lucy White b 9-8-1839 d 7-9-1923
   Confederate Soldier

Charles Smith White b 4-20-1849 d 7-6-1923

Ellen Scott w Charles Smith White b 12-5-1857 d 8-12-1916

Samuel Cowan Cason b 6-4-1886 d 6-9-1926   Served World
   War 9-15-1917 8-8-1919 in Postal Agency Attached A.E.F.

Theodore Hubert Furman b 10-5-1875 d 5-23-1920

Sarah Virginia dau A. M. & A. F. Reid b 4-19-1892 d 7-3-1893

A. M. Reid b 7-10-1855 d 2-5-1908

Lemuel W. Reid b 10-27-1884 d 9-26-1910

Infant dau J. R. & R. A. Glenn 6-9-1893

James Reid s J. R. & R. A. Glenn b 4-26-1898 d 6-8-1898

John Livingston Hill b 3-18-1849 d 9-27-1933

Susan Talulah Hill w J. L. Hill b 11-25-1852 d 12-8-1930

Minnie I. dau J. L. & S. T. Hill b 5-3-1891 d 1-23-1894

Infant children J. L. & S. T. Hill d 9-20-1893

Infant dau Mr & Mrs F. H. Graves

Floyd H. Graves d 11-23-1934 Aged 36 Years (Mortuary Marker)

Margaret Elizabeth Graves w J. S. Graves b 11-17-1835
   d 9-25-1899

LONG CANES CEMETERY

J. S. Graves b 1-22-1847 d 1-2-1905 Confederate Soldier

Sydney E. Graves b 1776 d 1909

Unmarked vault is near above. The following information
   was given by Mrs. J. T. Clinkscales, daughter of Mrs.
   Alice Crawford Graves: Mrs. Alice Crawford Graves w
   S. A. Graves b 11-27-1873 d 1-20-1930

Iva May dau S. A. & J. A. Graves b 5-21-1900 d 1-1-1904

J. Walter s Dr. L. T. & F. D. Hill b 7-13-1879 d 8-20-1884

Cadet Lieut. W. H. Hill b 7-15-1877 d 3-7-1896

Fannie Johnson Hill b 2-18-1860 d 2-17-1930

Lod T. Hill, M.D. b 5-12-1852 d 12-26-1922

Sarah Ella Hill (Mortuary Marker)

Rev. J. Lowrie Wilson, D.D. b 2-23-1839 d 7-9-1909
   Pastor Bethesda 1869-1885 Abbeville 1886-1909
   Officer CSA   Confederate Soldier

Rev. Claudius H. Pritchard S.C. Conf. M.E. Church South
   b 10-14-1821 d 3-5-1896   55 Years a faithful Ambassador
   for Christ.

Mary B. Pritchard w Rev. C. H. Pritchard d 7-8-1885
   Aged 59 Years 5 Mon 22 Days

Margaret Bowen dau Rev. C. H. & Mrs. M.B. Pritchard
   b 12-15-1854 d 4-30-1900

Mary Chapman dau C. H. & M. B. Pritchard b 3-21-1856
   d 7-18-1904

Mrs. F. E. White b 2-22-1820 d 3-7-1884

Mrs. Drucilla Eakin former wife Col. Donald Douglass
   d 11-17-1887 Aged 82 Years 2 Mon 7 Days

Tabitha M. Sherard b 6-30-1861 d 11-6-1920

William C. Sherard b 8-15-1851 d 2-15-1923

Lizzie C. Walker d 8-11-1885 Just Eighteen

Unmarked graves two adults near above, one is a Confederate
   Soldier.

Ladson Mills Perrin s Lewis & Ethel Mills Perrin b 6-11-1911
   d 3-19-1935

LONG CANES CEMETERY

Lewis Perrin b 11-12-1873 d 1-16-1936

Jas. T. s L. C. & H. A. Nickles b 6-22-1876 d 10-18-1876

Unmarked graves three adults near above.

John Maxwell Harden b 1-30-1847 d 3-25-1909 Confederate Soldier

N. T. Sassard d 3-3-1889 Aged 56 Years Confederate Soldier

Vernon s J. A. & M. J. King b 2-13-1894 d 9-12-1895

J. A. King b 7-10-1854 d 3-21-1924

Maggie Jane King w J. A. King b 5-14-1862

N. P. McIlwain b 9-6-1853 d 5-28-1920

John T. Young b 11-28-1855 d 11-28-1929

Miss Maggie Wadkins d 11-25-1926 Lived to a ripe Age

Sallie M. Watkins b 9-16-1826 d 1-29-1922

J. A. Watkins b 9-12-1858 d 7-3-1914

Nannie F.L. Watkins b 10-12-1862 d 6-19-1883

James W. Martin d 7-17-1936 Aged 73 Years

Sophia Helen Maxwell w Edward J. Harden b 2-29-1820
    d 11-12-1912

Infant dau J. A. & M. B. Smith b 10-26-1889

Mary B. Harden w J. Allen Smith b 2-17-1858 d 1-16-1899

J. Allen Smith b 3-4-1856 d 4-3-1931

Edward Harden Smith b 6-15-1896 d 7-1-1919 World War Veteran

Henry Gillespie Smith b 7-7-1880 d 6-13-1919

J. Allen s J. Allen Jr. & A. H. Smith b 10-17-1912 d 5-18-1915

John C. Ferguson b 4-26-1861 d 12-18-1915

Alice B. Ferguson w John C. Ferguson b 10-17-1864 d 9-17-1899

Pearl dau J. C. & A. B. Ferguson b 7-20-1888 d 8-20-1889

James Laval Martin b 1838 d 1922

Henrietta Stitt Martin b 1842 d 1922

LONG CANES CEMETERY

David Hugh Hill b 9-9-1884 d 6-16-1924

Infant s F. M. & Z. E. Wilson b & d 12-20-1891

Thomas Warren Allen b 1830 d 1895 Confederate Soldier

Sallie C. McCollum w Thomas Warren Allen b 1836 d 1909

Jones Fuller Miller b 1855 d 1923

Ione Allen w J. F. Miller b 8-14-1859 d 4-22-1904

Unmarked graves two infants near above.

Hettie McCollum b 1848 d 1925 dau John McCollum & Jane
  McKay

Isabella McKay b 1808 Cheraw, S.C. d 1885 Spartanburg, S.C.

S. Cora Allen dau T. W. & S. C. Allen b 10-2-1871 d 10-31-1887

William Terril Speed b 9-19-1858 d 3-3-1898

Fannie Ferguson Speed b 1-11-1870 d 12-12-1911

Thomas Ferguson b 3-5-1866 d 4-29-1908 Woodmen of World

Unmarked adult grave near above.

Blume Paslay s R. A. & Canie B. Richey b 8-1-1886 d 4-25-1897

Carrie B. Richey w R. A. Richey b 6-24-1862 d 8-17-1914

Robert A. Richey b 3-25-1864 d 1-16-1935 (Mortuary Marker)

Infant sons Hugh & Eva Bowen

W. G. Chapman b 3-4-1859 d 12-26-1914

James Calvert s J. C. & C. B. Thomson b 11-17-1912 d 6-6-1914

James Calvert Thomson b 1-23-1875 d 4-26-1935

Winona Durst w W. D. Barksdale b 10-25-1876 d 5-12-1911

Dale Barksdale Welsh b 3-18-1913 d 7-20-1934

Unmarked infant grave near above

Marie McNeill w C. F. McNeill b 12-1-1894 d 10-24-1917

Wm. M. Anderson b 11-26-1866 d 12-20-1929 Masonic Emblem

Virgil M. Waters d 7-23-1931 Aged 64 Years (Mortuary Marker)

LONG CANES CEMETERY

Unmarked adult grave near above.

Eula Mae Moss d 5-18-1929 Aged 18 Years 16 Days (Mortuary Marker)

Infant Mr & Mrs E. R. Wilson d 5-12/13-1933

Unmarked infant grave near above.

Infant c R. M. McCall d 5-2-1930 Aged 1 Day

Unmarked graves three adults & infants are near above.

Annie White w R. H. Greene b 1885 d 1914

Sara E. dau R. H. & Annie Greene 1914

S. Rachel Reagan b 3-18-1840 d 3-7-1902

Amanda E. Barksdale w J. H. Barksdale b 8-4-1844 d 3-16-1916

J. H. Barksdale b 7-1-1846 d 7-10-1922

Mattie Barksdale b 4-22-1885 d 4-1-1911

Edwin Y. Barksdale b 12-1-1874 d 9-9-1904

James H. s J. H. & A. E. Barksdale b 1-12-1889 d 7-4-1891

James Homer Oulla d 7-22-1935

James E. McIlwain b 8-6-1855 d 4-9-1908

Mrs. Anna Lou McIlwain d 4-2-1937 Aged 67 Years 6 Mon
   23 Days (Mortuary Marker)

Lucy J. dau T. L. & E. A. Moore b 11-2-1868 d 10-11-1891

George Clarence Reid b 1890 d 1918

Thomas Hoyt Reid b 1860 d 1920

Hannah Dusenberry Reid b 1861 d 1915

Unmarked infant grave near above.

Eunice dau J. B. & M. J. Sharp Aged 1 Year

Infant dau J. B. & M. J. Sharp

Jas. B. Sharp b 12-9-1853 d 9-7-1919

Mary J. Sharp w Jas. B. Sharp b 2-8-1857 d 8-1-1920

Robt. Samuel Gordon b 1881 d 1920 Woodmen of World

LONG CANES CEMETERY

Carl P. Sharp b 7-14-1897 d 9-2-1929

Maria Gibert w Pierre Gibert b 1823 d 1892

Pierre Gibert b 1820 d 1899

Elizabeth Gibert b 1849 d 1906

Jesse Carlisle Gordon b 6-14-1876 d 4-28-1932

J. P. Gordon b 11-4-1835 d 4-16-1917

Nancy E. Gordon w J. P. Gordon d 10-12-1883

Unmarked graves three adults near above.

Fannie E. Gordon w J. P. Gordon d 3-6-1887

John Pearson Billings b 1864 d 1933

Maggie R. Billings w J. P. Billings b 1-21=1862 d 10-24-1916

Katie dau J. P. & M. R. Billings b 12-2-1893 d 3-23-1896
  Aged 2 Year 3 Mon 21 Days

Jane L. Gordon b 7-30-1815 d 12-22-1902

Mary Watt Gordon b 4-1-1811 d 12-7-1893

R. T. Gordon b 6-20-1809 d 12-21-1887

Nellie Hill d 4-30-1897 Aged 17 Years

Nellie dau James A. & Bertha Hill b 7-16-1899

Lizzie Benson

Kittie Benson

Eva Benson

David Sloan Benson

David L. Benson d 1930 Aged 9 Days (Mortuary Marker)

Martin Govan Zeigler d 9-13-1888 Aged 58 Years
  Confederate Soldier

Lavinia A. Zeigler w M. G. Zeigler dau Rev. & Mrs. Saml.
  A. Dunwoody n 11-1-1830 d 6-30-1908

Jennie dau M. G. & L. A. Zeigler d 10-16-1892 Aged 23 Years

Benie dau M. G. & L. A. Zeigler d 7-12-1891 Aged 24 Years

Long Canes Cemetery

Henrietta Emory dau M. G. & L. A. Zeigler d 6-19-1883
  Aged 18 Years

Georgia Caroline dau M. G. & L. A. Zeigler d 6-11 1883
  Aged 22 Years

Samuel Jacob Zeigler b 8-19-1850 d 2-20-1928

John G. Edwards, M.D. b 1884 d 1931

John Gibson Edwards b 2-14-1832 d 8-23-1904 Confederate
  Soldier

Janie Amanda Bell w John G. Edwards b 10-3-1846 d 8-22-1921

Rosa Edmonia eldest dau J. G. & J. A. Edwards d 10-21-1883
  Aged 12 Years 2 Mon 13 Days

Joseph Calhoun Cason b 7-14-1890 d 7-30-1915

Elizabeth Cason b 1895 d 1896

Samuel C. Cason b 9-13-1852 d 2-13-1898

Hattie Allen w Sam'l. C. Cason b 10-10-1857 d 9-19-1887

Unmarked infant grave near above.

Ellen Ramey w C. Hughes d 6-14-1885 Aged 41 Years

Jesse D. 6-1885 Aged 10 Mon

Cicero Hughes b 9-10-1840 d 1-26-1914 Confederate Soldier

Aylett c James & Nena T. Chalmers d 6-11-1906 Aged 20 Mon

James Chalmers b 2-8-1862 d 4-1-1919

Christine Hadre dau Joseph T. & Carrie H. Hughes d 7-10-1914
  Aged 15 Mon

Rosa Ellen dau J. T. & Carrie H. Hughes b 4-25-1915 d 12-24-1916

Jacob Miller b 1815 d 8-16-1882 Confederate Soldier

Martha M. Miller w Jacob Miller b 11-19-1828

Lula L. dau W. P. & M. I. Wardlaw d 5-3-1874 Aged 2 Years 7 Mon

Unmarked adult grave near above.

Hassie M. Beacham d 6-12-1929 Aged 66 Years 4 Mon 4 Days
  (Mortuary Marker)

Belton Knox Beacham b 3-5-1855 d 11-4-1918

Unmarked infant grave near above.

George s L. W. & Mary H. White b 7-21-1881 d 2-11-1919

Infant s George & Nelle White 1-13-1913

Infant dau George & Nelle White 5-28-1917

Lambert Jones White b 2-9-1872 d 11-21-1898

Leonard Waller White b 7-7-1843 d 2-13-1907 Confederate
    Soldier

Mary Helen Jones w Leonard W. White b 9-20-1849 d 3-14-1932

Leonard Waller s L. W. & Mary H. White b 7-13-1884 d 4-27-1907

Helen O'Neall dau L. W. & M. H. White w Rev. E. D. Kerr
    b 3-27-1887 d 10-11-1914

Children of L. W. & M. H. White

Children of J. E. & E. K. Brickman

John Bonah White, M.D. b 1890 d 1-1930

R. M. Haddon b 12-29-1847 d 8-26-1924

Hannah Perrin w R. M. Haddon b 11-7-1844 d 9-27-1904

Isabel Perrin Haddon w Wm. E. Hill b 2-17-1875 d 12-22-1908

Unmarked adult grave near above.

R. B. Ferguson b 2-8-1862 d 6-17-1928

Georgia Ferguson w R. B. Ferguson b 5-6-1867

Andrew Stevenson b 10-22-1840 d 2-6-1896

William Stevenson b 12-24-1866 d 1-15-1901

Unmarked adult grave near above.

D. Lucien Mabry b 4-16-1888 d 3-30-1893

Unmarked adult grave near above.

Infant dau J. L. & E. B. Perrin b 12-13-1888 d 12-14-1888

Infant sons Mary P. & F. S. Hill

Mary Penney w F. S. Hill b 1875 d 1906

Unmarked infant grave near above.

W. T. Penney b 1839 d 1908 Confederate Soldier

Mary Shillito w W. T. Penney b 1838 d 1911

William Shillito Penney b 1879 d 1904

Robert Emmett Cox b 11-2-1892 d 9-9-1931

Unmarked graves four adults near above, one a Confederate
  Soldier.

John Robert s Samuel Clark & Amanda Shillito Link
  b 1-25-1881 d 1-9-1936

Willie Clark s S. C. & M. A. Link d 11-10-1882
  Aged 4 Years 1 Mon 6 Days

Samuel Clark Link b 10-10-1850 d 8-3-1934

Margaret Amanda Link w Samuel Clark Link b 5-3-1844 d 2-7-1932

Willa Lou dau L. & M. Link b 12-7-1925 d 3-17-1926

Lindsay Stevenson s T. & M. Link d 6-5-1919
  Aged 1 Year

Mary Virginia Reid w G. C. Dusenberry b 10-18-1852 d 7-30-1921

Margurite dau Rev. M. W. & Margaret Gordon b 6-22-1901
  d 10-9-1901

W. A. Calvert b 11-3-1867 d 1-15-1926

Mary E. Botts w W. A. Calvert b 4-25-1868 d 3-11-1922

Mary L. dau W. A. & M. E. Calvert d 8-9-1894 Aged 2 Mon

Estelle dau W. A. & M. E. Calvert b 5-15-1895 d 11-9-1885

Donald Hill s W. A. & M. E. Calvert b 11-7-1909 d 9-15-1917

Charles Leonard Calvert b 11-8-1900 d 12-27-1930

Alfred W. Fant b 11-4-1873 d 2-6-1927

Dolly dau F. & C. C. Fant d 1-13-1892 Aged 20 Years

Cornelia C. Fant w F. Fant b 9-6-1845 d 2-8-1923

Fielding Fant b 8-24-1844 d 5-26-1902

James Gibert Hamilton b 9-2-1844 d 2-18-1912

Elizabeth M. Hamilton d 11-10-1924 Aged 80 Years 10 Mon 30 Days
  (Mortuary Marker)

LONG CANES CEMETERY

Willie Douglass Purdy b 2-11-1866 d 10-29-1928

Unmarked adult grave near above.

Adolphus W. Jones b 4-11-1857 d 9-27-1924

Celia T. Miller w Adolphus W. Jones b 10-29-1857

Frank M. McDavid b 6-12-1912 d 11-21-1930

Frank B. Jones d 8-11-1934 Aged 53 Years (Mortuary Marker)

H. P. McIlwain b 1-22-1883 d 5-5-1909 Masonic Emblem

H. P. McIlwain b 8-3-1845 d 7-15-1904

Ella Westfield McIlwain b 2-26-1856 d 2-19-1919

Thomas Beggs s H. P. & E. V. McIlwain d 12-22-1889
  Aged 18 Mon 2 Days

Warren T. Cochran b 2-24-1842 d 1-26-1891

J. Benjamin Cochran b 5-17-1834 d 3-18-1900 Confederate Soldier

Mary C. Cochran b 8-18-1843 d 5-20-1917

William L. Cochran b 1-26-1874 d 1-28-1914

Unamrked graves two adults near above.

Alpheus E. Lesly b 2-2-1834 d 3-23-1905 Confederate Soldier

Virginia Miller w Alpheus Lesly b 8-15-1839 d 4-15-1892

Unmarked graves three adults near above.

Sgt. John W. Lesly Co A 2 S.C. Rifles CSA Confederate Soldier

Unmarked adult grave near above.

A. H. s F. D. & N. Sorrow b 11-22-1907 d 12-21-1909

Infant sons J. W. & L. M. Sorrow b 2-10-1907 d 2-11/21-1907

Unmarked infant grave near above.

L. B.

George Leeper Cochran d 5-4-1937 (Mortuary Marker)
  Aged 58 Years 9 Mon 13 Days

Margaret E. Cochran d 5-20-1928 Aged 56 Years 2 Mon 29 Days
  (Mortuary Marker)

Unmarked adult grave near above.

Jefferson D. Winn h Adolphie Winn b 6-8-1860 d 1-7-1909
    m. 12-2-1884

Infant dau J. D. & M. A. Winn b & d 7-7-1890

Paul D. s Mr & Mrs J. D. Winn b 5-24-1901 d 4-3-1902

J. B. Winn b 1-4-1866 d 1-11-1928

Mary Elizabeth Winn w J. B. Winn d 6-20-1896 Aged 26 Years

Nannie R. dau J. B. & M. E. Winn b 7-26-1890 d 3-16-1904

Robert L. Winn b 12-25-1863 d 2-14-1909

Jessie Winn b 6-9-1864 d 9-13-1926

Infant dau R. L. & J. P. Winn b 10-22-1894 d 10-29-1894

William T. King b 11-29-1859 d 10-3-1929

Alice Sutherland w William T. King b 2-27-1864

Corrine dau W. T. & A. King b 3-25-1898 d 6-2-1901

Annie Bell dau W. T. & Alice King b 4-5-1899 d 8-7-1899

Lewis L. s W. T. & A. King b 9-22-1891 d 5-6-1893

Infant dau W. T. & A. King b 10-16-1900 d 2-2-1901

Unmarked grave of infant near above.

Samuel W. Cochran b 11-22-1824 d 9-3-1893   Confederate Soldier

Hannah Maria Means w Samuel W. Cochran b 2-4-1834 d 2-20-1928

Margaret Hannah dau C. M. & M. E. Cochran 12-2-1906

P. S. Rutledge d 12-1-1884 Aged 77 Years

Unmarked infant grave near above.

Paul DeLisle Mazyck b 1857 d 1897

John Fraser Livingston s P. DeL. & S. L. Mazyck b 5-28-1893
    d 3-6-1895

Frances Livingston dau P. DeL. & S. L. Mazyck b 5-11-1887
    d 10-3-1894

Samuel Gilmer b 11-3-1797 d 5-22-1873

Elizabeth Jane Gilmer w Samuel Gilmer b 6-22-1826 d 3-25-1901

Unmarked graves two adults near above.

Otto Edwin s O. E. & H. D. Lindford b 3-21-1899 d 5-19-1900

Joseph Henry Latimer b 1848 d 1899 Confederate Soldier

Lou Ella Cozby w Joseph Henry Latimer b 1852 d 1935

Daniel H. Howard   Co F 24 SC Inf CSA

Hugh Wilson d 8-24-1899 Aged 85 Years   Masonic Emblem

Unmarked graves two adults & infant near above.

John P. Garrison b 1863 d 1923

Unmarked grave three adults, one a Confederate Soldier
  near above.

Kate Schroeder w James C. Cox b 8-30-1868

James C. Cox b 3-1-1863 d 3-20-1925

Unmarked graves two adults near above.

Wade Samuel Cothran b 12-6-1859 d 1-17-1921

Cornelia Brunson Cothran w Wade Samuel Cothran b 6-6-1870
  d 7-31-1920

William A. Willson b 1-7-1881 d 6-16-1924

Unmarked grave of adult near above.

James Clifton McMillan b 10-9-1896 d 11-15-1897

James Leslie McMillan b 2-2-1865 d 4-26-1928

Otto Bristow b 10-14-1886 d 11-12-1935

Unmarked infant grave near above.

Mary Elizabeth Isaacs w J. H. Isaacs b 5-13-1837 d 12-20-1897

Nina A. Isaacs w G. W. Syfan b 10-29-1864 d 12-27-1929

Unmarked graves two adults & infant near above.

Bennie F. s E. J. & Nora Lawton b 9-23-1916 d 5-22-1918

Dock E. s L. W. & Josie Johnson b 4-20-1891 d 8-27-1903

Unmarked infant grave near above.

LONG CANES CEMETERY

L. W. Johnson b 9-17-1847 d 11-30-1906

James Homer Sorrow b 7-3-1900 d 8-12-1900

Unmarked graves two adults & infant near above.

Worth Lamar s John D. & Ruth L. Jennings b 5-30-1896
    d 12-16-1897 Aged 1 Year 6 Mon 17 Days

Infant dau John D. & Ruth L. Jennings b & d 2-7-1900

W. H. Confederate Soldier

Jennie Bone w Ernest O. Wilson b 10-27-1878 d 8-27-1906

William J. Perry b 7-2-1884 d 10-21-1918

James A. Perry b 1-17-1892 d 6-9-1913

Unmarked graves five adults near above.

Florence dau C. B. & L. O. Wosmansky b 8-4-1905 d 8-5-1905

Lucile dau C. B. & L. O. Wosmansky b 2-1-1901 d 6-11-1901

Mary F. Milford w W. T. Milford b 11-10-1858

W. T. Milford b 6-12-1839 d 3-5-1899 Masonic Emblem

W. H. Gaston b 8-10-1836 d 1-13-1909 Member Co G 4th SC Regt.
    Member Baptist Church Confederate Soldier

Louise Ione dau Sims A. & Alice I. Allen b 4-18-1892
    d 2-12-1912

Sims Anderson Allen b 5-11-1850 d 5-22-1922

William D. Melton b 1849 d 1918 Masonic Emblem

Sarah E. Melton w W. D. Melton b 7-12-1855 d 9-19-1915

Unmarked adult grave near above.

Infant s W. D. & S. E. Melton

J. T. s T. F. & H. H. Uldrick

Miss Ruby Mae Uldrick d 4-2-1936 Aged 37 Years (Mortuary Marker)

Mamie Milford b 1-29-1860 d 10-22-1928 w N. P. Milford

N. P. Milford b 6-14-1853 d 9-30-1926

James Carlisle s C. P. & U. Hammond b 10-14-1900 d 12-5-1900

Unmarked graves five adults near above.

Susie L. Willson w LeRoy T. Miller b 12-2-1866 d 10-8-1920

LeRoy T. Miller b 11-28-1866 d 2-9-1926

Matthew Harvey Wilson b 7-29-1848 d 9-25-1911 Confederate Soldie

Frank A. Wilson b 12-2-1825 d 6-12-1900

Sarah A. Wilson w Frank A. Wilson b 8-7-1833 d 2-16-1901

Birdie Wilson w Wade H. Wilson b 11-16-1876 d 11-28-1934

Cora Pritchett Paschall b 8-22-1894 d 8-12-1936

J. R.F. Willson b 2-2-1930 d 10-7-1900

Sarah M. Wilson b 12-27-1834 d 6-27-1914

James M. Ellis b 5-28-1884 d 9-2-1885

Bessie M. Ellis b 3-9-1886 d 10-27-1888

William R. Ellis b 9-9-1887 d 9-13-1888

Mary E. Ellis b 7-23-1863 d 2-2-1934

William R. Ellis b 8-9-1861 d 2-1-1934

Christianna K. Ellis b 4-21-1862 d 2-21-1904

Christianna D. Ellis b 2-10-1904 d 6-24-1904

Anna Virginia Ellis dau Mr & Mrs R. L. Ellis b 3-26-1918
    d 6-2-1934

Infant s U. B. & M. J. Uldrick b 11-19-1900 d 4-17-1901

Infant dau U. B. & M. J. Uldrick b 11-19-1900 d 5-1-1901

Julia M. dau W. B. & M. J. Uldrick b 11-13-1902 d 6-17-1904

W. B. Uldrick b 6-4-1862 d 3-4-1925

Martha Jane Winn w W. B. Uldrick b 3-16-1868 d 12-19-1917

Margaret dau T. S. & O. C. Milford b 3-5-1903

Sgt. John B. Wilson b 1833 d 1913 Confederate Veteran

Unmarked graves of adult & infant near above.

Lucina M. McMahan b 4-9-1851 d 8-21-1917

LONG CANES CEMETERY

P. A. McMahan b 6-29-1847 d 3-4-1901

Mary Holcomb w James Taggart b 3-27-1854 d 7-20-1922

James Taggart b 2-4-1851 d 3-1-1918

Mamie E. Taggart w Joe T. Hughes b 5-2-1880 d 7-1-1902

Amarilous Holcomb w W. H. Holcomb b 7-4-1824 d 3-3-1900

Infant s Herman & Winton Benton 5-20-1916

Hal Taggart b 1-4-1883 d 7-2-1923

Mary Jane McMahon b 7-25-1850 d 9-8-1932

T. C. McCord b 1-8-1860 d 1-24-1913 Woodmen of World

Thomas B. McCord b 8-13-1826 d 5-15-1902

Willie Clarence McCord b 12-24-1896 d 12-15-1898

Olla Mae McCord b 6-22-1900 d 5-15-1902

Eliza McCord b 8-30-1889 d 3-28-1906

Charles Joseph Lyon b 11-4-1864

Martha Elizabeth w Charles Joseph Lyon b 12-23-1867
    d 10-29-1927

William Henry Lyon b 11-2-1887 d 9-17-1928
    World War Veteran

Anna Ethridge w C. Shrine b 8-14-1866 d 4-8-1928

Unmarked graves two infants near above.

Reuben Jones d 4-12-1931 Aged 22 Years 9 Mon (Mortuary Marker)

Sarah Ann Jones b 1-4-1856 d 4-27-1926

Lewis P. Ferguson d 2-25-1921 Aged 40 Years 25 Days
    (Mortuary Marker)

Frank L. s J. Y. & Ora Turman b 7-11-1900 d 11-7-1900

Julia M. dau J. Y. & Ora Turman b 5-13-1904 d 6-12-1905

James Milton s J. Y. & O. Turman b 9-1-1908 d 6-16-1917

James M. Strawhorn b 8-31-1849 d 1-22-1917

Infant dau Mr & Mrs J. M. Strawhorn 5-16-1921

Unmarked graves three infants near above.

Mattie Amelia Moss b 8-26-1885 d 6-11-1928

Unmarked infant grave near above.

M. Edwin Willson b 1843 d 1917

G. E. Wilson b 1842 d 1928

Unmarked adult grave near above.

Sara Nancy Harrison d 9-14-1932 Aged 4 Years Old
   (Mortuary Marker)

William H. Lewis b 10-3-1873 d 11-3-1914

James s J. N. & M. E. Lewis   8-15-1931

Mary J. Bowie w J. W. Bowie b 5-9-1874 d 7-11-1915

Ruth dau J. W. & M. J. Bowie 7-6-1915

Joseph B. Jr. s J. B. & A. L. Bowie 3-31-1922

Claudie Willie Long b 1-13-1913 d 5-10-1914

Jane Elizabeth Henry w F. L. Morrow b 9-24-1847 d 6-24-1921

Florence Rebecca Henry b 11-13-1856 d 3-26-1913

Maggie Leona Sprouse w John L. Bruce b 6-13-1882 d 6-21-1917
   Woodmen Circle

Infant s I. E. & R. G. Sprouse b 3-27-1920 d 4-15-1920

Unmarked graves adult & infants near above.

Charles A. Botts d 12-31-1928 Aged 43 Years 10 Mon
   (Mortuary Marker)

Janie Bell Edwards b 7-5-1897 d 11-19-1926

Julia Elizabeth dau R. S. & Lucia G. Mundy b 12-10-1925
   d 11-23-1926

Annie B. Getsinger d 1-2-1929 Aged 45 Years 1 Mon 2 Days
   (Mortuary Marker)

J. T. Simmons b 7-27-1876 d 11-23-1929

Cassie Simmons b 4-17-1872 d 10-28-1931

Unmarked infant grave near above.

LONG CANES CEMETERY

Infant of C. A. Fleming d 8-16-1930 (Mortuary Marker)

John H. Sharpe b 1877 d 1930

James William Sharpe b 5-10-1859 d 1-14-1917

Sarah Malinda Henry b 7-29-1859 d 7-15-1935

J. W. Boyd b 10-19-1878 d 5-20-1915 "Dry your tears
  dear Jessie"

Infant s Mr & Mrs J. W. Boyd d 6-9-1915

Unmarked adult grave near above.

James Ben Boyd d 5-16-1925 Aged 15 Years 5 Mon 21 Days
  (Mortuary Marker)

Euranca Fortescue b 3-8-1912 d 4-16-1931

Ophelia Fleming w W. T. Fortescue b 11-2-1875 d 10-6-1933

W. J. Milford b 5-6-1857 d 7-5-1925

Lonie Thomas dau W. J. & Mamie Milford b 6-11-1909 d 5-11-1915

Martha Frances dau Mr & Mrs C. T. King b 2-20-1914 d 1-4-1915

Eva Marguerite dau R. S. & E. F. Woodhurst b 9-5-1929 d 1-18-1931

George W. Milford d 2-28-1936 Aged 76 Years 8 Mon 15 Days
  (Mortuary Marker)

Unmarked infant grave near above.

Mrs. Mary Ann McIlwain d 8-25-1934 Aged 75 Years 6 Mon 10 Days

Benjamin C. McIlwain b 1851 d 1916

Unmarked adult grave near above.

Clementine Hon Tongie w J. A. McIlwain b 4-17-1856 d 12-20-1912

Jas. Andrew McIlwain b 11-27-1849 d 5-14-1919

Emity Augusta dau L. R. & I. B. Willson b. 9-22-1891 d 11-21-1911

Unmarked graves two adults near above.

Langdon Cheves Haskell b 7-13-1860 d 7-1-1929

Kate Calhoun w L. C. Haskell b 11-8-1861 d 8-17-1916

Ella Wardlaw dau L. C. & K. C. Haskell b 12-19-1887 d 1-17-1919

Cheves Haskell Fair b 8-9-1927 d 11-4-1927

Edwin Calhoun s Edward & Frances Middleton Calhoun
  Member Co C 6th SC Cav CSA, wounded Travillians, Va.
  6-12-1864. b 1-21-1839 d 8-26-1917

Sarah Smarr Tilman w Edwin Calhoun dau Edward & Kitty
  Calhoun Tilman b 5-25-1843 d 4-5-1911

Arthur Wardlaw Calhoun b 1872 d 1917

Miss Frances M. Calhoun d 12-18-1933 Aged 66 Years
  (Mortuary Marker)

Luther H. Nickles b 3-8-1873 d 2-2-1909

Infant s Wm. H. & Edna H. White 1-7-1918

Robert Gordon Hagen b 1-9-1865 d 7-14-1934

Emma Holliday Hagen w Robert Gordon Hagen b 12-21-1869
  d 1-5-1935

Frank s R. G. & E. L. Hagen b 4-28-1910 d 7-16-1910

Anna Mundy w W. R. Mundy b 9-2-1856 d 3-18-1913

Wm. Robt. Mundy b 6-4-1841 d 5-28-1914 Co G Orr's Rifles
  1861-1864 Confederate Soldier

W. A. Stevenson b 12-6-1864 d 8-20-1930

2nd Lieut. Wm. Oscar Stevenson s Wm. A. & Mary R. Stevenson
  b 11-5-1890 d 10-8-1918 buried Bellicourt, France, Bony
  Aisle Grave 123, row 5 plot C American Cemetery 636.
  Distinguished & exceptional gallantry of The American
  Expeditionary forces, awarded him by citation, John J.
  Pershing, Commander-in-Chief.

Annie Evelyn dau W. A. & M. R. Stevenson b 2-16-1907
  d 2-15-1908

Samuel Link s Mr & Mrs Jno. A. Wilson b 12-31-1914 d 7-4-1915

Henry Latimer s Mr & Mrs Jno. A. Wilson b 12-22-1907 d 12-22-190

John A. Wilson d 11-9-1928 Aged 71 Years 7 Mon 28 Days
  (Mortuary Marker)

Infant dau W. H. & A. L. Mundy b 4-5-1911

Henry M. Mundy d 6-18-1929 Aged 21 Years (Mortuary Marker)

Mrs. Ada Lee Mundy d 3-9-1929 Aged 55 Years 29 Days
  (Mortuary Marker)

LONG CANES CEMETERY

Unmarked graves of adult & infant near above.

Lety C. Wright w James W. Wright b 10-27-1833 d 2-24-1913.

J. W. Wright b 2-12-1838 d 11-1-1919 Masonic Emblem

W. T. Wright b 5-22-1873 d 5-30-1914 Masonic Emblem

Unmarked grave of adult near above.

Thomas Edgar Link b 10-31-1892 d 4-27-1926

Susan C. Link b 1865 d 1915

Miss Grace Link d 5-21-1936 Aged 34 Years 6 Mon 21 Days
   (Mortuary Marker)

Horace s T. H. & M. Finley b 2-9-1911 d 2-19-1913

Sallie May Lavina dau T. H. & M. Finley b 11-2-1918
   d 5-2-1919

Frederick Lamar s T. H. & M. Finley b 12-5-1919 d 9-14-1920

Unmarked infant grave near above.

James L. Finley d 6-26-1930 Aged 2 Mon 26 Days

Infant s Clifton & Idona Sprouse 6-24-1931

Infant dau Mr & Mrs E. W. Hunt b & d 4-28-1915

Mary Helen dau W. S. & M. J. Gordon b 1-1-1913 d 5-24-1915

James Perrin s Mr & Mrs L. P. Edwards b 9-27-1929 d 6-1-1931

Augustus Marshall Smith b 11-16-1867 d 3-2-1928

Unmarked graves two adults near above.

Emma dau James & Permelia McIlwain b 8-30-1856 d 10-3-1926

G. E. McIlwain b 11-14-1853 d 4-30-1935

Infant s J. R. & Kate C. McIlwain 11-24-1920

Virginia Hagen McIlwain & Infant McIlwain d 10-9-1914

J. W. Nichols b 1855 d 1917

Elizabeth Nichols w J. W. Nichols b 1851 d 1920

Claude L. Cochran b 1877 d 1914

J. W. s Charles C. & Lucie E. Nabors b 1906 d 1914

Frances C. Coleman b 3-9-1852 d 1-14-1912

W. F. McCord b 7-22-1849 d 10-15-1932

Annie Black w W. F. McCord b 10-7-1866

John R. Wilson Jr. d 6-5-1928 Aged 1 Year 8 Mon 4 Days
(Mortuary Marker)

Rachel Ramona Wilson d 4-8-1931 Aged 1 Year 8 Mon 10 Days
(Mortuary Marker)

Kathern M. Wilson d 12-12-1927 Aged 2 Days (Mortuary Marker)

Wallace G. Wilson b 2-28-1870 d 1-14-1913

Ida Eskin McCord b 1-8-1873 d 3-13-1936 Woodmen Circle

Thomas Wesley McCord b 11-25-1851 d 6-11-1931

William C. Simmons b 9-20-1886 d 9-25-1930

William T. Simmons b 5-20-1854 d 1-18-1924

Mattie F. Wade w W. T. Simmons b 12-2-1856 d 12-25-1917
Aged 61 Years 23 Days

Annie Ruth dau W. D. & Sallie Simmons b 8-17-1908 d 4-22-1911

Fred D. Simmons b 8-12-1878 d 4-30-1929

Infant of David Simmons d 3-11-1929 Aged 16 Hours
(Mortuary Marker)

Alexander Goode Faulkner b 5-3-1860 d 6-1-1911 Woodmen of World

Unmarked adult grave near above.

H. Klugh Eskin b 6-28-1886 d 10-10-1918

Edgar S. Eskin b 11-24-1890 d 10-4-1918 in France
323 Inf Co. F 81 Div

Samuel T. Eskin b 1-19-1848 d 12-26-1934

Jennie B. Eskin w Samuel T. Eskin b 12-2-1850 d 6-28-1925

H. Burnet Eskin b 3-8-1879 d 10-13-1918

Eunice F. dau H. B. & Gena Eskin b 4-11-1905 d 6-22-1906

Unmarked infant grave near above.

S. T. Eskin b 9-9-1880 d 11-23-1928

Duayne Hill s R. E. & Jennie M. Cox b 10-23-1909 d 10-28-1918

Robert Emmett Cox b 5-14-1866 d 10-10-1914

Mary Harbeson dau R. E. & S. J. Cox b 9-10-1907 d 5-4-1910

Mrs. Sudie F. Quain d 2-19-1933 Aged 35 Years (Mortuary Marker)

Joe B. Ferguson d 8-29-1932 Aged 70 Years 7 Mon 10 Days
(Mortuary Marker)

Fannie May dau Mr & Mrs J. B. Ferguson b 3-4-1893 d 2-3-1909
Aged 15 Years 11 Mon

Luetta dau H. M. & S. F. Mundy b 12-20-1909 d 5-3-1910

Unmarked graves two infants near above.

Hugh M. Mundy b 12-10-1857

Sarah F. Mundy w Hugh M. Mundy b 8-22-1865 d 3-18-1923

John Andrew Harris b 12-11-1859 d 2-5-1907

Annie Coogler w John A. Harris b 10-7-1868 d 3-4-1924

W. W. Harris d 7-26-1932 Aged 45 Years World War Veteran
(Mortuary Marker)

Bessie Wilson w R. Y. Simmons b 10-26-1882 d 8-4-1916

Leroy s Robert & Bessie Simmons b 8-15-1909 d 10-16-1909

Robert Y. s Robert & Bessie Simmons b 4-19-1906 d 6-27-1907

Jane Eleanor McKee w G. N. Nickles b 5-3-1850 d 9-26-1919

Susan R. Wilson w L. W. Dansby b 2-7-1866 d 7-28-1912

Infant s A. B. & Virginia M. Cochran 5-1906

Mary G. Cochran b 12-15-1902 d 5-21-1904

Augustus B. Cochran b 9-13-1871 d 5-26-1936

Hubert s Wm. N. & Ada Graydon b 3-4-1900 d 1-15-1904

Norwood Graydon d 10-16-1919 Aged 22 Years (Mortuary Marker)

William Norwood Graydon d 8-3-193? Aged 70 Years 7 Mon 23 Days
(Mortuary Marker)

McMillan Graydon d 10-12-1928 (Mortuary Marker)

Lety dau T. C. & M. C. McDowell b 2-11-1904 d 2-18-1904

LONG CANES CEMETERY

Infant of S. O. McDowell d 8-22-1922 (Mortuary Marker)

Sam O. McDowell d 11-1-1929 Aged 17 Years 5 Mon 23 Days
(Mortuary Marker)

Wesley Clayton s W. D. & Mary C. Ferguson b 11-18-1896
d 3-16-1912

Infant s W. D. & Mary C. Ferguson 5-18-1904

W. C. F.

Gracie dau J. D. & N. E. Kirby b 11-3-1895 d 2-14-1905

Unmarked infant grave near above.

Lizzie Sprouse d 5-16-1922 Aged 58 Years

Edward Lee Herndon b 1883 d 1908

Sallie Scott d 7-3-192? Aged 58 Years (Mortuary Marker)

Unmarked adult grave near above.

Marion W. Russum d 1-5-19?? Aged 5 Mon (Mortuary Marker)

Talmadge W. Russum D 1-20-1931 Aged 1 Year 5 Mon 1 Day
(Mortuary Marker)

Edward C. Herndon d 6-18-1930 Aged 1 Year 6 Mon 8 Days
(Mortuary Marker)

Unmarked infant grave near above.

Andrew J. Ferguson b 1-7-1868 d 4-8-1932

Thos. A. Stallings b 4-19-1866 d 10-27-1931

T. H. Cochran b 8-14-1907

Martha Cochran Bowen b 6-17-1857 d 6-1-1929

Thomas B. Eskin b 9-9-1870 d 1-28-1915 Woodmen of World

John T. s T. B. & M. L. Eskin b 8-26-1900 d 1-21-1911

G. R. Richardson b 11-20-1850 d 4-12-1910

John A. s G. R. & M. Richardson b 3-18-1878 d 2-12-1906

W. E. Gordon d 7-28-1933 Aged 66 Years 3 Mon 15 Days

Unmarked infant grave near above.

A. F. Calvert b 2-8-1848 d 9-17-1918 Confederate Soldier

Unmarked adult grave is near above.

Natalie A. dau G. E. & L. C. Calvert b 10-30-1907 d 5-24-1908

Myrthis H. dau G. W. & M. J. Cochran b 9-17-1877 d 8-15-1909

G. W. Cochran b 12-21-1849 d 11-21-1914

Infant s S. E. & C. C. Nance b 4-17-1911 d 4-19-1911

Sarah E. dau D. E. & M. R. Nickles b 11-19-1902 d 8-17-1909

D. E. Haddon b 6-30-1850 d 5-24-1920

Infant s B. A. & O. M. Uldrick b & d 1-21-1910

Victorine dau D. D. & M. R. Hall b 4-3-1888 d 8-25-1909

Paul Eugene Hall d 4-12-1937 Aged 46 Years (Mortuary Marker)

Unmarked graves two adults & infants near above.

Louise Reid Wilkes b 1-3-1886 d 1-26-1920

Infant s R. C. & L. R. Wilkes 5-8-1916

Unmarked grave of adult near above.

H. H. Maxwell b 12-26-1855 d 7-16-1910

Infant dau T. H. & S. E. Maxwell 2-28-1906

Elizabeth dau T. H. & S. E. Maxwell b 9-15-1908 d 12-30-1908

Infant dau J. E. & F. G. Bailey b 9-3-1907 d 10-15-1907

Bennie A. s W. D. & Annie Smith b 5-15-1915 d 1-31-1917

Walter David Smith d 1-19-1926 Aged 56 Years (Mortuary Marker)

Unmarked adult grave is near above.

Mary E. McDorman d 7-21-1927 (Mortuary Marker)

Henry Watson d 12-14-1929 Aged 3 Mon 12 Days (Mortuary Marker)

Unmarked graves three infants near above.

Charlie Powell b 1909 d 1910

Gracie Powell 1912

John H. Huiskamp b Jaassen Guelders, Holland 10-4-1855
  d Abbeville, SC 9-28-1911

Infant s J. L. & L. M. Burrell b & d 1-9-1910

Sarah E. dau W. T. & I. M. Strawhorn b 1-22-1908 Aged 7 Mon

William Lucious Able b 7-17-1887 d 10-23-1935

Ruby Norrell Able b 9-4-1908

James William Tribble b 10-18-1883 d 6-28-1924 Masonic Emblem

Irene W. Tribble b 10-1-1888 d 8-6-1923

William Radford Tribble b 4-27-1919 d 1-4-1920

Infant dau Mr & Mrs J. W. Tribble Born Dead

Infant dau Mr & Mrs J. H. Whaley Born Dead 3-11-1908

Emmie Joan dau J. C. & E. W. Gaston b 2-23-1930 d 6-3-1930

Infant of E. B. & L. C. Busbee d 12-18-1904

Grace B. dau E. B. & L. C. Busbee b 3-6-1906 d 12-20-1906

W. Claud Lanier d 9-27-1936 Aged 65 Years (Mortuary Marker)

Pierce s Pierce & Mallie I. Bowen b 3-26-1906 d 12-1-1906

Mrs. Caroline Miller McAllister d 7-18-1935 Aged 56 Years
   3 Mon 25 Days (Mortuary Marker)

John V. Schroeder b 6-29-1835 d 1-3-1905 Masonic Emblem

Eliza C. Brooks w J. V. Schroeder b 12-9-1841 d 5-23-1917

Nancy P. DuPre b 12-11-1880 d 11-23-1918

Frank DuPre d 9-1-1922 Aged 19 Years (Mortuary Marker)

F. A. DuPre d 3-30-1925 Aged 48 Years (Mortuary Marker)

Augustus B. Schroeder b 10-15-1875 d 8-21-1907

Unmarked graves two infants near above.

Janie Sharpe Strawhorn b 11-19-1878 d 6-14-1934

Frances Inez Strawhorn b 1-15-1904 d 3-27-1904

James Vernon Simpson d 10-31-1933 (Mortuary Marker)
   Aged 34 Years 2 Mon 26 Days

Charles M. Bradberry d 7-30-1932 Aged 3 Mon 28 Days
   (Mortuary Marker)

LONG CANES CEMETERY

Raford E. Stewart d 9-14-1936 Aged 8 Years (Mortuary Marker)

Unmarked adult grave near above.

Miss Isabell Moore d 8-18-1928 Aged 25 Years 17 Days
  (Mortuary Marker)

Unmarked graves two adults near above.

Robert W. Borders b 1893 d 1923

Henry Marsh Dellinger Jr. d 4-23-1925 Aged 7 Years 11 Mon 23 Days

Unmarked adult grave near above.

Walter Derden b 6-9-1893 d 7-2-1929 World War Veteran
  Masonic Emblem

Claud H. Woodhurst b 7-9-1910 d 8-24-1936

Shirley B. White b 7-1-1879 d 10-30-1923 Woodmen of World

Jack Turner Loftis d 11-2-1924 Aged 8 Mon 8 Days (Mortuary Marker)

Mary Loftis Aged 37 Years 6 Mon (Mortuary Marker)

Unmarked graves World War Veteran & infant near above.

Margaret Malisa C. Dansby d 2-6-1935 Aged 73 Years
  (Mortuary Marker)

William F. Dansby d 4-21-1927 (Mortuary Marker)

Florence Wilson w J. L. Sprouse b 12-13-1884 d 8-2-1925

Andrew Hagan Jackson b 12-1-1892 d 10-12-1925 World War Veteran

James Preston s Mr & Mrs J. A. Woodhurst b 3-2-1917 d 1-1-1925

Unmarked graves of adult & infant near above.

Marie Wilson w W. J. Wilson d 3-18-1926 Aged 29 Years

Alma J. Wilson d 4-16-1931 Aged 32 Years 3 Mon 25 Days
  (Mortuary Marker)

Ruth E. dau W. J. & Marie Wilson b 2-25-1917 d 6-2-1930

Ben Alexander Thomerson b 12-21-1902 d 7-20-1926
  S.C. Seaman 201 US Navy World War Veteran

J. H. Thomerson d 11-28-1932 Aged 76 Years 11 Mon 8 Days
  (Mortuary Marker)

Unmarked adult grave near above.

LONG CANES CEMETERY

Elizabeth King w Rev. Thomas Wharey, D.D. b 1843 d 1927

Unmarked infant grave near above.

Joseph Hutchinson d 10-1-1926 About 4 Years (Mortuary Marker)

Unmarked graves two adults near above.

James C. Nickles b 10-19-1895 d 10-27-1924

Lillie Haddon Nickles b 8-10-1863 d 6-1-1934

Thomas Eskin Nickles b 7-14-1900 d 9-20-1934

Elizabeth dau W. D. & Naomi Hood b 2-28-1923 d 2-27-1924

Unmarked infant grave near above.

Nellie Clark w C. H. Bosdell b 6-2-1893 d 12-9-1924

L. R. Clinkscales b 11-29-1892 d 5-27-1924

Elizabeth O. Clinkscales b 6-23-1887 d 6-17-1924

Eva M. Clinkscales b 11-14-1869 d 8-16-1929

Julian Mann Wilkinson b 3-15-1889 d 10-26-1929 World War Veteran

Claude P. Wilkinson b 4-9-1896 d 1-25-1926

Dora Morrow w M. C. Rosenberg b 4-29-1848 d 7-7-1926

Mrs. W. L. Dawson d 11-1934 Aged 64 Years (Mortuary Marker)

William L. Dawson d 1-22-1937 Aged 68 Years (Mortuary Marker)

Unmarked graves two infants near above.

Samuel Mims s Frederick Cason & Alice Mims Cason b 6-23-1902
    d 5-23-1905

Infants of Mr & Mrs J. C. Burns d 2-24/25-1934 (Mortuary Marker)

Unmarked infant grave near above.

Susan Ferguson w L. B. Ramey b 6-6-1885 d 8-16-1925

Unmarked infant grave near above.

Elsie Ray dau Thomas & S. E. Robison b 6-27-1921 d 8-27-1923

William D. Beauford d 6-17-1935 Aged 76 Years 4 Mon 8 Days
    (Mortuary Marker)

Mary Creswell Beauford d 6-3-1935 Aged 74 Years 9 Mon 14 Days
    (Mortuary Marker)

Billie s T. C. & Emmie Purdy b 1922 d 1923

Unmarked graves of adult & two infants near above.

Charles David Cowan b 11-6-1872 d 7-27-1935 Woodmen of World

Unmarked adult grave near above.

A. Thomas Hall b 3-23-1862 d 10-22-1936

Unmarked adult grave near above.

Mary Dawson Bell b 2-1895 d 2-10-1929

Mrs. Janie H. Hollingsworth d 8-19-1934 Aged 76 Years 5 Mon
    19 Days (Mortuary Marker)

Unmarked adult vault near above.

Ernest W. Douglass d 1-12-1932 Aged 20 Years 4 Mon 28 Days
    (Mortuary Marker)

John David Nickles b 6-24-1886 d 7-9-1924

Sara Estelle dau John David & Estelle Stevenson Nickles
    b 9-12-1924 d 9-30-1924

Claude Prighet Cromer b 6-25-1894 d 5-18-1922
    Soldier of his Country 7 Years World War Veteran

Nina Orr Beauford w Claude P. Cromer b 4-19-1893

H. B. Cannon b 4-18-1862 d 11-10-1921

Infant dau Robert M. & Esther Fleming Stevenson 8-8-1921

Thomas H. Botts b 7-17-1872 d 7-10-1921 Masonic Emblem

Jennie McCord w Thomas H. Botts b 5-9-1874 d 3-12-1932

Marguerite dau T. S. & N. W. White 5-23-1918

James R. White d 5-29-1934 Aged 71 Years 1 Mon 29 Days
    (Mortuary Marker)

Ellen Howie w Robt. Howie b 1852 d 1926

Elizabeth Howie dau T. V. & C. A. Howie 1912

Unmarked graves three adults near above.

J. R. Owens b 12-24-1854 d 3-18-1930 Aged 76 Years 2 Mon 22 Days

Clyde Ernest Yoder b 10-13-1883 d 10-10-1921

Miss Frances Elizabeth Sharp d 7-1-1934 Aged 54 Years 11 Mon 15 Days (Mortuary Marker)

Mary LeRoy dau James R. & Lizzie L. Evans b 1916 d 1930

J. A. Stevenson b 4-25-1862 d 1-17-1932

Lulie Reid Stevenson b 11-18-1863 d 3-3-1933

Andrew Thomas McIlwain b 9-3-1848

Jane Brice w Andrew Thomas McIlwain b 6-19-1851 d 3-21-1929

William A. McIlwain b 9-16-1872 d 12-6-1921

T. Huber McIlwain b 1889 d 1918

Arthur A. McIlwain d 4-2-1929 Aged 46 Years 10 Mon 6 Days (Mortuary Marker)

M. B. Syfan b 3-11-1869 d 4-4-1933

Mamie Cochran w M. B. Syfan b 6-26-1870

Miss Hannah M. Cochran d 11-12-1932 Aged 86 Years (Mortuary Marke

Samuel H. Cochran b 5-23-1844 d 7-4-1917 Confederate Soldier

Infant s M. B. & Grace Cochran 3-18-1929

R. William s T. M. & Eugenia Cochran b 6-10-1922 d 3-6-1925

Mamie Christine Blanchett b 6-15-1922 d 9-22-1935

Edward W. Milford b 11-5-1894 d 1-29-1929

Margaret Smith d 4-6-1937 Aged 6 Years (Mortuary Marker)

Arthur Lawton d 3-19-1937 Aged 3 Years (Mortuary Marker)

Nathan Lawton d 5-24-1937 Aged 4 Years (Mortuary Marker)

Mary Louise Shurnat d 11-10-1935 Aged 6 Mon 15 Days (Mortuary Marker)

Henry Harold Laughlin d 5-24-1930 Aged 3 Mon 20 Days (Mortuary Marker)

Annie Lee w J. Dave Lawton b 5-15-1886 d 5-17-1926 Aged 37 Years

Elise B. Sharpe b 5-7-1887 d 2-21-1936

Ruth C. Ellis b 11-10-1894 d 2-25-1918

Nellie M. Ellis b 9-26-1891 d 4-26-1923

LONG CANES CEMETERY

Unmarked infant grave near above.

Raymond s J. T. & L. B. Norris d 11-1-1919 Aged 7 Mon

Unmarked adult grave near above.

Anna Grant w E. M. Osborne b 12-3-1868 d 2-16-1929

Thomas Byrd Osborne b 12-31-1895 d 8-16-1919

James H. Bell b 12-10-1848 d 8-8-1927 Confederate Soldier

Markus S. s Joe & Ellen Langford b 3-18-1871 d 9-7-1919
  Masonic Emblem

Unmarked adult grave near above.

James S. Banks b 10-4-1869 d 1-11-1920

Unmarked graves two adults near above.

J. H. Link b 4-12-1852 d 2-5-1924

Sarah Ann Link b 7-9-1858 d 7-4-1936

Unmarked infant grave near above.

Hubert C. Cox d 8-22-1934 Aged 37 Years World War Veteran
  (Mortuary Marker)

Lemuel Kenneth s S. M. & Fannie Strawhorn b 3-25-1928
  d 12-9-1933

D. Emory Newell b 3-2-1879 d 12-23-1934

Sanford O'Neil Ethridge d 5-23-1937 Aged 59 Years (Mortuary Marker)

Alice E. Ethridge d 3-18-1934 Aged 53 Years 9 Mon 21 Days
  (Mortuary Marker)

Infant dau J. W. & M. J. Strawhorn b 9-9-1907 d 9-10-1908

Charles Stone d 6-22-1935 Aged 10 Mon 3 Days (Mortuary Marker)

Mrs. Edith L. Nickles d 2-1935 Aged 57 Years 7 Mon 16 Days
  (Mortuary Marker)

R. S. Uldrick

Mrs. Addie Mae Mundy d 8-1-1932 Aged 38 Years 5 Mon
  (Mortuary Marker)

Carrie Uldrick dau Mr & Mrs C. C. Uldrick (Mortuary Marker)

Unmarked infant grave near above.

LONG CANES CEMETERY

Ralph Edwin s Mr & Mrs W. W. Simpson b 1935 d 1936

Carl Stone Jr. d 4-28-1932 Aged 6 Years 11 Mon 24 Days
   (Mortuary Marker)

William R. Sprouse b 3-24-1884

Cora Lee Sprouse b 2-15-1892 d 10-21-1936

Dock F. Andrews Co G 14 SC Inf CSA

Memorial on front gate entrance, Long Cane Cemetery 6-27-1935
   "In Memory of Veterans of Eight Wars who are buried in this
   Cemetery"

Bradley, Hiram Tusten 59
  James Foster 11
  M. T. 59
  W. W. 59
Branch, Annie 35
  Elizabeth 35
  F. 35
  Fanny (Mrs.) 35
  Frances 35
  I. (Dr.) 35
  Isaac (Dr.) 35
  Samuel 35
  W. T. 35
  William Tully 35
Brickman, E. K. 70
  J. E. 70
Bristow, Otto 74
Brogden, A. 1
  A. L. 1
  Kenneth 1
Brooks, Corrie J. (Mrs.)
  39
  Elizabeth 39
  J. H. 40
  J. W. 39
  J. W. (Capt.) 39
  L. M. 40
  Leunie Walter Thomas
    14
  Paul 40
  S. A. 39
  Sallie 39
  Willie Walter 13
Brown, Norma Elizabeth 59
  Samuel 7
  Sarah Wideman 40
Bruce, John L. 78
  Maggie Leona Sprouse
    78
Brunson, J. J. 61
Buchanan, E. (Mrs.) 34
  Margaret (Mrs.) 20
Burdett, James H. 2
Burns, J. C. (Mr.) 88
  J. C. (Mrs.) 88
Burrell, J. L. 86
  L. M. 86
Busbee, E. B. 86
  Grace B. 86
  L.C. 86
Butler, J. C. 6
  James Chalmers 6
  S. C. 6
  S. P. 6
  Sara Emma 6
Calhoun, Arthur Wardlaw
  80
  Edward 80
  Edwin 80
  Frances M. (Miss) 80
  Frances Middleton 80
  J.A. 15
  James 15
  James Caldwell 15
  John A. 15
  John Alfred 15
  Martha Maria 14
  Sarah 15
  Sarah M. 15
  Sarah N. 15
  Sarah Smarr Tilman 80
  W. N. (Corp.) 15
Calvert, A. F. 84
  Annie Mary 45
  Charles Leonard 71
  D. C. 45
  Donald Hill 71
  Estelle 71

Calvert (cont.)
  G. E. 85
  James M. 45
  Jas. M. 45
  John W. 18
  L. C. 85
  Lucinda Moore 45
  Lucy L. 45
  M. 45
  M. E. 71
  M. I. 45
  Mary E. Botts 71
  Mary L. 71
  Nancy D. 45
  Natalie A. 85
  W. A. 71
Campbell, Claude 8
  Lillie 8
  Mary Agnes 8
Canfield, Addie 10
  E. V. 10
  M. Cornelia 10
Cann, Alice 4
  Dolly Blanchett 8
  M. B. 4
  Mary E. 4
  N. C. 4
  O. L. 3
  Obie 4
  Ralph 4
  Thos. Lester 8
  W. T. 4
Cannon, H. B. 89
Carroll, Bennie F. 3
  G. W. 12
  Geo. W. 12
  Ida T. DuPre 12
  J. M. 3
  John W. 12
  Katie 3
  M. 3
  Ralph 3
Cason, Alice Mims 88
  B. H. 8
  E. G. 8
  Earl Gilleland 8
  Elizabeth 69
  Ellen Wright 7
  Frederick 8
  Hattie Allen 69
  Joseph Calhoun 69
  Sam'l C. 69
  Samuel C. 69
  Samuel Cowan 63
  Samuel Mims 88
Chalmers, A. W. (Dr.) 34
  Alex. 33
  Aylett 69
  C. 33
  Christina Ramey 33
  Frances (Mrs.) 34
  J. D. 33
  James 69
  James D. 33
  Nena T. 69
  Richard 33
Chapman, W. G. 66
Cheatham, J. B. 6
  J. Earnest 6
  Janie B. 6
  Janie Britt
  R. B. 6
Cheek, J. A. 16
  John A. 16
  L. R. 16
  Louis Robertson 16
Chiles, James Mabry 45
Christian, Mary Ann 49

Christian (cont.)
  Mary Louisa 49
  T. M. 49
  Thomas M. 49
Clark, Alexander W. 8
  Dila W. 56
  James 3
  John L. 4
  Mary E. 56
  Ola 3
  W. L. 3
  Watson J. 4
Clary, Lula Blackwell
  Hutchinson 6
  W. F. 6
Clemans, Mary Ellis
  (Mrs.) 26
Cleves, Langdon 13
Clinkscales, Elbridge R.
  (Capt.) 10
  Elizabeth O. 88
  Ella A. Kay 12
  Eva M. 88
  J. T. (Mrs.) 64
  James F. 12
  John Franklin 12
  John T. 6
  John Thompson 6
  L. R. 88
  Lamar 8
  Milford 8
  Ruth Edwards 6
  Sudie 6
  Sudie Nance 6
Cobb, Edmond 34
  Elizabeth Clisby 34
  Elizabeth Medley
    (Mrs.) 34
  James Medley 34
Cochran, A. 34
  A. B. 83
  A. G. 62
  A. V. 49
  Agnes Gilmer 49
  Augustus B. 83
  Aylett Chalmers 33
  C. M. 73
  Caroline Etna 49
  Clara Gay 61
  Claude L. 81
  Eugenia 90
  Fannie Eugenia 62
  G. W. 85
  George Leeper 72
  Grace 90
  Hannah M. (Miss) 90
  Hannah Maria Means 73
  J. Benjamin 72
  J. S. 33, 34
  Lizzie 62
  M. E. 73
  M. J. 85
  Margaret E. 72
  Margaret Hannah 73
  Mary C. 72
  Mary G. 83
  Mary Sue 49
  Myrthis H. 85
  R. H. 49
  R. William 90
  Robert H. 49
  Samuel H. 90
  Samuel W. 73
  Samuel W. (Sr.) 43
  T. H. 84
  T. M. 90
  Virginia M. 83
  Warren T. 72

Greene (cont.)
  R. H. 67
  Sara E. 67
Greer, Thomas Mc. 28
Griffin, J. F. 22
  Susan G. 22
  Tellula Elizabeth 22
Grubb, James Robert 7
Gunter, W. H. M. (Mr.) 3
  W. H. M. (Mrs.) 3
Hadden, Francis Lavinia
  20
  Isaac (Rev.) 20
  Jane 20
Haddon, B. M. 35
  Calvin 59
  D. E. 85
  E. J. 59
  Hannah Perrin 70
  Ida 59
  Lula H. 35
  R. B. 59
  R. M. 70
Hagen, E. L. 80
  Emma Holliday 80
  Frank 80
  R. G. 80
  Robert Allen 61
  Robert Gordon 80
Haigler, Sarah Harris 8
Hall, A. L. 1, 3
  A. Thomas 89
  Ada 1, 3
  Curtis H. 1, 3
  D. D. 85
  H. H. 35
  M. B. 35
  M. R. 85
  Paul Eugene 85
  Sloan A. 58
  Victorine 85
Hamiton, A. C. (Capt.) 17
  Alexander C. 17
  Andrew M. 18
  Andrew (Maj.) 18
  Delphia Alelia 17
  Elizabeth G. 34
  Elizabeth M. 71
  Elizabeth Wharton 52
  James Gibert 71
  Jane 18
  Jane (Mrs.) 18
  John A. 34, 52
  Louis Davis 34
  Nancy 34
  Richard A. 17
  William 34
Hamlin, A. B. 9
  L. M. 9
  Mary F. 4
Hammond, A. E. 61
  Arthur S. 55
  Barney V. 55
  C. P. 75
  C. V. 55
  Fannie 55
  Frank D. 55
  H. Scott 61
  J. S. 61
  James Carlisle 75
  Jimmie 55
  Joseph Harold 61
  Kate 61
  M. P. 55
  Mary Rutledge 55
  U. 75
  W. S. 61
Harden, Edward J. 65

Harden (cont.)
  John Maxwell 65
  Sophia Helen Maxwell
    65
Harris, Annie Coogler 83
  James Bolick 5
  John A. 83
  John Andrew 83
  M. B. 5
  Mary Bolick 4
  W. H. 5
  w. w. 83
Harrison, Agnes 49
  E. H. 2
  E. T. 49
  Edna Tusten 49
  F. E. 49
  Francis E. (Dr.) 49
  Lina Lee 2
  M. B. 2
  Sara Nancy 78
Haskell, Allen Wardlaw
  13
  Charles Thomas 13
  Charles Thomson 13
  Charlott 13
  Ella Coulter 47
  Ella Wardlaw 79
  K. C. 79
  Kate Calhoun 79
  L. C. 79
  Langdon Cheves 79
  Mary Sophia 47
  Sophia Lovell 13
  William Thomson 13
Haygood, Emily 24
  W. W. 24
Hemphill, Eugenia 5
  Jessie Culver 5
  Robert 5
  Robert Grier 5
  Robert Reid 5
Henderson, Francis (Jr.)
  37
Henry, A. Mc.(Jr.) 18
  A. McIlwaine 18
  Albert 18
  F. 18
  Florence Rebecca 78
  Frances 27
  Francis 18
  Frank 18
  J. 27
  John Thomson 18
  Margaret Ann 27
  Mary 28
  Peter 27, 28
  Rebecca 27, 28
  S. C. 18
  S. E. 18
  Sarah Ellen Hill 18
  Sarah Malinda 79
  William 27
Herbert, Hattie S. 35
  Hattie Shand 35
  Thomas G. (Rev.) 35
Herndon, Edward C. 84
  Edward Lee 84
Hicks, Isdora 9
  Joseph 9
Hill, Anna H. 18
  Bertha 68
  Bessie 60
  David Hugh 66
  Elizabeth Clark 59
  F. D. 64
  F. S. 70
  Fannie Johnson 64

Hill (cont.)
  Isabel Perrin Haddon
    70
  J. L. 63
  J. Walter 64
  James A. 68
  John Livingston 63
  L. T. (Dr.) 64
  Lod T. (M. D.) 64
  M. C. 60
  Mary (Mrs.) 25
  Mary Chapin Moore 60
  Mary P. 70
  Mary Penny 70
  Mary Thomson 18
  Mattie Ward 18
  Minnie I. 63
  Nellie 68
  R. E. 18
  R. M. 60
  Robert E. 18
  Robert Emmett 18
  Robert McGowan 59, 60
  S. T. 63
  Samuel Lane 59
  Sarah Ella 64
  Sarah J. 18
  Susan Talulah 63
  W. H. (Cad. Lt.) 64
  Wm. 18
  Wm. E. 70
Hinton, J. H. 2
  Maud 2
  May 2
Hodges, Milton Jackson 9
Holcomb, Amarilous 77
  W. H. 77
Holliday, Eli 36
  Emma 36
  Mary A. 36
Hollingsworth, Janie H.
  (Mrs.) 89
Hollinshead, J. 53
Holman, Nancy (Mrs.) 38
Hood, Elizabeth 88
  Naomi 88
  W. D. 88
Horn, Hardy 50
Horton, Crattie Lue 1
  T. M. 1
Hotzclaw, Susan Elizabeth
  1
Howard, Daniel H. 74
Howie, C. A. 89
  Elizabeth 89
  Ellen 89
  Robt. 89
  T. V. 89
Howlet, Margaret 25
Hughes, B. P. 42
  Benjamin P. 42
  C. 69
  Carrie H. 69
  Christine Hadre 69
  Cicero 69
  Claude E. 11
  E. H. 48, 49
  E. V. 11
  Ellen Ramey 39
  G. P. 11
  J. T. 69
  Jane C. 42
  Jane Cornelia 42
  Joe T. 77
  Johnny Dunn 42
  Joseph T. 69
  Mamie E. Taggart 77
  Rosa Ellen 69

Hughes (cont.)
  S. E. 48
  Sarah E. 48
  Thomas 48
  William H. 49
  William P. 42
Hughey, E. I. (Mrs.) 34
  William M. 34
Huiskamp, John H. 85
Hunsucker, Huey 1
Hunt, E. W. (Mr.) 81
  E. W. (Mrs.) 81
Hunter, Henry Edmund 11
  John A. 17
  John Edward 11
  Joseph Franklin 11
  Margaret Jane 11
  Mary Katherine 11
  Nancy Glasgow 11
  Sarah Elizabeth 11
  William Andrew (M. D.)
    11
  William Washington 11
Hutchinson, Joseph 88
Hutto, James F. 54
  Stella Douglass 54
Irwin, Elizabeth 25
Isaacs, J. H. 74
  Mary Elizabeth 74
Jackson, Andrew Hagan 87
  Ann Rebecca 43
  Eliza 43
  J. E. 56
  J. Edward 56
  M. E. 56
  Thomas 43
James, E. P. 4
  J. B. 4
  J. M. 4
  John M. (Jr.) 4
  Mary 4
  William J. 4
  Willie 4
  Willie Ansel 4
Jennings, John D. 75
  Ruth L. 75
  Worth Lamar 75
Johnson, Dock E. 74
  Frances 62
  Josie 74
  L. W. 74, 75
  Lornena 62
  W. E. 62
  Walter Eugene 62
Jones, Adolphus 72
  B. W. 51
  Celia T. Miller 72
  Frank B. 72
  Ida G. Johnson 51
  Joe E. 51
  Mary 51
  Reuben 77
  Robt. 51
  Sarah Ann 77
Karey, Robert W. 25
Keaton, William P. 44
Keller, Davis Marcus 1
  J. W. (Dr.) 51
  J. W. (M. D.) 51
  James Wesley 51
  L. R. 51
  L. R. (Mrs.) 51
  Mary S. 51
  Susan A. Wilson 51
  W. W. 1
  Willie Isaac 51
Kerr, Amos Davis 56
  E. D. (Rev.) 70

Kerr (cont.)
  H. S. 42
  Helen O'Neall 70
  Henrietta 56
  John Davis 56
  Leontina (Mrs.) 42
Kidd, Allen 4
Killingsworth, Corrie M.
    7
  S. F. (Dr.) 7
  S. F. (Mrs.) 7
  Samuel F. 7
Kinard, Lola A. White 59
  T. E. 59
King, A. 73
  Alice 73
  Alice Sutherland 73
  Annie Bell 73
  C. T. (Mr.) 79
  C. T. (Mrs.) 79
  Corrine 73
  Dessie 54, 55
  Dessie Gillan 55
  Essie Jane 55
  F. A. 55
  Fannie A. 55
  Florence Annie 55
  G. Thomas 55
  J. A. 65
  J. D. 54, 55
  Jane C. 55
  Lewis L. 73
  M. J. 65
  Maggie Jane 65
  Martha Frances 79
  Vernon 65
  W. Sloan 55
  W. T. 73
  William T. 73
Kirby, Gracie 84
  J. D. 84
  J. R. 2
  M. O. 2
  Marion 2
  N. E. 84
  Roland 2
Kirkwood, Hannah 20
  Hugh 20
Klugh, C. B. 11
  Caroline 11
  Charles B. 11
  Emma E. 32
  J. C. 11
  James Coke 11
  P. D. 32
  Pascail Daus 32
Knox, Della 44
  John 44
  Mary C. Moore 44
Kurg, Jacob 61
Kyle, James 33, 34
  Jane A. 33
  Jane Louisa 34
  N. C. 34
  Nancy 34
  Nancy Eliza 33
  Sarah Virginia 34
  W. H. 34
Landrum L. 5
  W. W. 5
Langford, Ellen 91
  Joe 91
  Markus S. 91
Langley, C. K. 10
  Carrie K. 10
  Collie 9
  Collie P. 9, 10
  E. E. 61

Langley (cont.)
  Edmund B. 10
  J. B. 10
  J. F. 61
  Jack Keith 9
  Mary Alice 61
  Mary E. 9
  Norma C. 10
  Norman H. 10
  W. M. 9
  William Meadors 9, 10
  Wilma Whatley 10
Lanier, W. Claud 86
Latimer, Joseph Henry 74
  Lou Ella Cozby 74
Laughlin, Henry Harold 90
Lawson, F. J. 31
  Fannie J. 31
  Frances Jane Shillito
    31
  H. W. 31
  Hiram W. 31
  Lucy Wardlaw 31
  Sallie 31
Lawton, Annie Lee 90
  Arthur 90
  Bennie F. 74
  E. J. 74
  J. Dave 90
  Nathan 90
  Nora 74
Leach, Percy James 7
Lee, Ben Robert Augustus
    16
  Charles Francis 16
  John Jinkins (M. D.)
    16
  Thomas (Dr.) 54
  William Augustus 16
Lesly, Alpheus 72
  Alpheus E. 72
  Augustus 32
  Cornelia R. 33
  David 33
  Eliza M. 33
  Elizabeth 33
  James L. 33
  John W. (Sgt.) 72
  Liuwellin L. 32
  Louisa (Mrs.) 33
  Martha 32
  Martha E. 32
  Robert Hall 33
  Robert L. 32
  Thomas 32
  Virginia Miller 72
  William A. 32
  Wm. 32
  Wm. E. 32
Lester, R. L. 50
Lewis, J. N. 78
  James 78
  M. E. 78
  William H. 78
Liddell, Eliza Ann 21
  Eliza Ann Davis 21
  George 21
  Hattie Turner 57
  James 21
  Jas. T. (Capt.) 57
  John 21
  Louisa Ramsay 57
  Sarah 21
  Sarah Hartgrove 21
  Thomas Cunningham 57
Linford, H. D. 74
  O. E. 74
  Otto Edwin 74

Link, Amanda Shillito 71
  E. T. 49
  Emily Mary Schuck 60
  Emma E. 49
  Grace (Miss) 81
  Grace Smith (Mrs.) 44
  J. H. 91
  John Robert 71
  L. 71
  Leila T. 45
  Leila Thomson Quarles
    44
  Lindsay Stevenson 71
  M. 71
  M. A. 71
  Mamie Lawson 60
  Margaret Amanda 71
  Robt. S. 60
  S. C. 71
  S. J. 45
  S. Jenner 44
  Samuel Clark 71
  Sarah Ann 91
  Susan C. 81
  T. 71
  Thomas Edgar 81
  Willa Lou 71
  Willie Clark 71
Lipford, A. F. 34
  Carl Warner 34
  V. F. 34
Little, Arra T. 38
Livingston, Clara Amanda
  28
  Donald H. 28
  Henry 29
  J. F. 28
  J. F. (1st Lt.) 28
  J. Fraser 28
  Jno. F. 28
  John F. 28
  John Frazier (Dr.) 28
  Julia McCaw 28
  M. F. 28
  Margaret A. 28
  Mary 29
  Sarah A. 28
  William Donald 28
Loftis, Jack Turner 87
  Mary 87
Lomax, David K. 5
  Eliza 36
  G. W. 5
  George W. 5
  James 43
  Julia 5
  Lucien H. 43
  M. E. 5
  M. Eliza McIlwain 5
  Martha J. 36
  Mary E. 5
  Mary Elizabeth 43
  Mary Norwood 15
  William 36
  William James 15
  Wm. 36
Long, Claudie Willie 78
  Ida Allen 49
  John J. 10
  Lula 10
  W. H. 49
Lovell, Sophia 13
Lucas, E. R. 15
  Edwin R. 15
  James Perrin 15
  M. R. 15
  Mamie N. Perrin 15
Lynch, A. W. (Dr.) 17

Lynch (cont.)
  Dora 17
  Elizabeth 17
Lyon, Charles Joseph 77
  Elizabeth 41
  Elizabeth Cowan 41
  Frances Eugenia 41
  H. B. 41
  H. T. 41
  H. T. (Dr.) 41
  Harriet B. Dendy 41
  Harvey T. 41
  J. A. 41
  J. Fuller 5
  James Fuller 5
  John 11
  John T. 41
  Joseph 41
  Joseph W. 41
  Margaret Elizabeth 11
  Marie Louise Pelletier
    5
  Martha Elizabeth 77
  Samuel 41
  Sarah J. 41
  William Andrew 5
  William Henry 77
  Willie H. 41
Lythgoe, George
  Berkenhead 18
  Hannah 19
  John Wier 19
McAllister, Caroline
  Miller (Mrs.) 86
McBride, E. H. 52
  Pearlie Parker 52
McBryde, Adam 37
  Andrew 37
  John 37
  Susan 37
  Susan H. (Mrs.) 37
McCall, R. M. 67
McCaslan, Margaret Susan
  11
  Patrick H. 11
McCaw, Julia C. 28
  Mary 28
McClellan, John 25
McClinton, Sarah 41
  Wm. 41
McClung, Charles
  Alexander (Capt.)
    21
  Chas. A. 56
  Corrie Miller 21
  Mary Yarbrough 21
  Rufus Morgan 21
McCollum, Hettie
  Jane McKay 66
  John 66
McCombs, H. 25
  Hannah 25
  Mariah 25
  W. 25
  William 25
McConnel, Elizabeth 46
McCord, A. M. 59
  Annie Black 82
  Eliza 77
  Essie 57
  I. N. 57
  Ida Eskin 82
  Jerusha 53
  M. L. 59
  Margaret Elizabeth
    Stevenson 59
  Nellie 59
  Olla Mae 77

McCord (cont.)
  T. C. 77
  T. W. 57
  Thomas B. 77
  Thomas Wesley 82
  W. F. 82
  W. L. 59
  William L. 59
  Willie Clarence 77
McCracken, William L. 39
McCraven, John 33
McCree, Agnes 20
McCurry, H. E. 9
  John W. 9
  Kinard L. 9
  Lilla I. 9
  M. G. 9
  M. S. 9
  Margaret Mililda
    Campbell 9
  Mattia S. 9
  Schalon A. 9
  W. A. 9
McDavid, Frank M. 72
McDill, Jasphere Virginia
  Delph 5
  Jefferson Hayne 5
  Jefferson Haynie 5
  William Andrew 5
McDonald, Leila Anderson
  42
  Matthew 43
  W. T. 42
McDorman, Mary E. 85
McDowell, Lety 83
  M. C. 83
  S. O. 84
  Sam O. 84
  T. C. 83
McFare, Nancy 24
McGowan, Alexander 47
  Lewis 47
  Samuel 47
  Sarah Wardlaw 47
  Susan 47
  Susan C. 47
  Susan Caroline 47
  William Campbell 15
McIlwain, A. T. 24
  Andrew 18
  Andrew Thomas 90
  Anna Lou (Mrs.) 67
  Arthur A. 90
  Benjamin C. 79
  Clementine Hon Tongie
    79
  Deborah Armon 20
  E. V. 72
  Edward 20
  Eliza 19
  Ella Westfield 72
  Emma 81
  G. E. 81
  H. P. 72
  J. A. 79
  J. B. 24
  J. R. 81
  James 81
  James E. 67
  Jane 19
  Jane Brice 90
  Jas. Andrew 79
  John 19
  Kate C. 81
  Mary 20
  Mary Ann (Mrs.) 79
  Mary Jane 46
  N. P. 65

Nance (cont.)
C. C. 85
F. E. 62
J. A. (Jr.) 10
Jeannette 62
John A 10
S. E. 85
S. F. 62
Samuel F. 62
Navy, Edward M. 35
Elizabeth 35
John E. 35
Neil, Elizabeth 19
Neuffer (Dr.) 6
(Mrs.) 6
Annie Hemphill 6
C. V. 6
G. A. (Dr.) 6
Gottlob A. (Jr.) 6
J. R. 6
Marie Louise 6
New, Blanche Inez 12
C. C. 3, 12
Katie 3
Katie (Mrs.) 3
M. B. 3, 12
Mary E. C. 3
S. A. 3
S. H. 3
Tommie Allen 3
Newell, D. E. 51
D. Emory 91
J. W. 51
John Andrew 61
L. W. 51
M. A. 51
Margaret A. Uldrick 51
Mary S. 55
Sarah A. 51
Wm. T. 55
Nichols, Elizabeth 81
J. W. 81
Nickles, D. E. 85
Edith L. (Mrs.) 91
Estelle Stevenson 89
G. N. 83
H. A. 65
James C. 88
Jane Eleanor McKee 83
John David 89
Jas. T. 65
John R. 61
L. C. 65
Lillie Haddon 88
Luther H. 80
M. R. 85
Sara Estelle 89
Sarah E. 85
Thomas Eskin 89
Nixon, William 1
Noble, Belle 16
Edward 16
Mary Battrey 16
William Bratton 16
Norris, J. T. 91
L. B. 91
Raymond 91
Norwood, Amelia Churchell 13
Amelia Walker 13
Ellen Frost Parker 16
Fannie N. Townsend 39
Henry H. 16
Henry Hester 16
J. P. 39
J. P. (Mrs.) 39
James A. 15
James Alexander 14, 15

Norwood (cont.)
John Samuel 13
Lila 15
Louisa H. M. Patterson 39
Nanita Perry 13
Sallie M. 39
Sarah 15
Sarah Hester 14
Sarah Mourin 15
W. C. (Dr.) 39
W. R. 39
W. T. 39
Wesly C. (M.D.) 39
Williamson 15
Willie Glover 14
Osborne, Anna Grant 91
E. M. 91
Thomas Byrd 91
Oulla, James Homer 67
Owen, A. 33, 34
Annie 40
David T. 40
J. T. 26
L. E. (also see Owen, T. E.) 33
Lucy 12
Martha Ann Wideman 40
Mary McCaslin 33
Matthew C. 59
Moses T. 40
Moses Taggart 40
S. E. 26
T. E. (also see Owen, L. E.)33, 40
Thomas E. 40
W. E. 12
William Edgar (Jr.) 12
Owens, J. M. (Rev.) 7
J. R. 89
Jesse M. (Rev.) 7
Lucius L. 7
Marthena C. 7
Parker (also see Foulke) 15
Allen Wardlow 14
Clarissa Annie Fleming 15
Edward (M. D.) 16
Edward Eugene 16
Edward Frost 14, 15
Edwin 16
Ellen Frost 14
Ellen Legare 15
Eller Elizabeth 14
Eugenia Calhoun 16
Eugenia G. 16
Julia DeVeaux 15
Lisa DeVeaux 15
Lucea Garvey 14
Lucia G. 14
Lucian G. 14
Margaret Wardlow 14
Margaretta A. 15
Mary W. Thomas 16
Rosalie Simkins 14
Sarah Allen 14
Thomas 14, 15
Thomas Drayton 16
Thomas Fleming 15
William C. 16
William Calhoun 16
William H. 14
William Henry 14
Parthemas, Jim 12
Paschall, Cora Pritchett 76
Paslay, Andrew 41

Patterson, M. E. 9
Mary E. McCurry 9
Mary Elender 9
W. B. 9
William B. 9
Pearl, Ola 24
Pennal, William R. 9
Penny, Mary Shillito 71
W. T. 71
William Shillito
Perrin, Amanda E. 22
E. B. 70
Ethel Mills 64
Eunice C. 44
Francis Hugh 48
Hannah Clarke 48
J. L. 70
J. W. 50
J. Wardlaw 50
James M. 44
James M. (Col.) 44
Jane E. 22, 47, 48
Jane Eliza 48, 50
Jane Wardlaw 63
Joel S. 44
Kittie C. 44
Ladson Mills 64
Lewis 51, 64, 65
Lewis Clarke Clopton 50
Lewis Wardlaw 48
Lewis Wardlaw (Jr.) 48
Mary Campbell 50
Mary E. 44
Mary Elizabeth 44
Mary J. 50
Mary McCaw 48
Mary Means 48
Robert C. 48
Tho. C. 22
Thomas 47
Thomas C. 48
Thomas Chiles 44, 48, 63
Thomas Samuel 47
Thos. C. 48
William Henry 47
Wm. F. 57
Perry, J. T. 46
James A. 75
William J. 75
Pool, Margaret V. Cunningham 43
Wm. R. (Capt.) 43
Porter, J. A. 10
M. A. 10
Mary Adline 10
William Robert 10
Posey, Agness Sarah 37
B. L. 17
B. V. 37
Benjamin V. 17
Martha A. 17
Mary (Mrs.) 17
Sarah 17
Powell, Charlie 85
Gracie 85
Power, Ella 6
Eva Dorn 6
W. L. 6
Pressly 61
H. E. 11
John Ebenezer (M. D.) 61
M. B. 11
Price, B. F. 56
Corrie 56

Price (cont.)
Hattie Black 56
James L. 56
M. C. 56
Mary A. 56
S. E. 56
Pritchard, C. H. 64
C. H. (Rev.) 64
Claudius H. (Rev.) 64
M. B. 64
M. B. (Mrs.) 64
Margaret Bowen 64
Mary B. 64
Mary Chapman 64
Purdy, Billie 89
Emmie 89
T. C. 89
Willie Douglass 72
Quain, Sudie F. (Mrs.) 83
Quarles, M. T. 27
Mary T. 27
May 27
T. P. 27
Thomas Perrin 27
Quay, A. 22
Raines, C. M. 5
Cora M. 5
J. C. 5
Jas. Bratton 5
Mary Lee 5
Ramey, L. B. 88
Susan Ferguson 88
Reagan, S. Rachel 67
Reese, Ella Eugenia
Bradley 7
H. D. 7
Henry Dodson 7
Milton Bradley 7
Reid, A. F. 63
A. M. 40, 63
George Clarence 67
Hannah Dusenberry 67
Hugh 21
J. A. 62
James A. 62
James C. 40
L. 40
Lemuel 40
Lemuel W. 63
Lizzie 40
Margie Elizabeth 62
S. W. 40
Samuel 40
Sarah Virginia 63
Sophia W. White 40
Thomas Hoyt 67
Richardson, G. R. 84
John A. 84
M. 84
Richey, Blume Paslay 66
Canie B. 66
Carrie B. 66
Elizabeth N. 41
Elmina 41
John B. 41
Margaret D. 17
R. A. 66
Robert 17, 36
Robert A. 66
William 17
Riley, William G. 6
Robertson, Agnes Baker 16
Eugenia Miller 16
F. M. 58
Frank M. 58
J. Townes 16
J. William 16
James Townes 16

Robertson (cont.)
Kitty Frances Dansby
58
Mary 24
Thomas 24
Robinson, Alice Eugenia
61
Andrew 21
Andy B. 61
Edward 20
Jane 41
John 20
L. A. 61
Leila A. 61
Mary Jane 61
Samuel 20, 41
T. J. 61
Robison, Elsie Ray 88
S. E. 88
Thomas 88
Roche, B. M. 40
Bethia M. 40
E. 42
Edward 43
Katherine A. 42
Lula C. 42
Lula Cheatham 42
M. B. 39
M. D. 39, 40
Margaret E. 43
Mary A. 43
Mary Anne 40
Maurice D. 40
Moses Owen 39
Patrick 42
Patrick A. 42
S. A. 42
Sallie 42
Sarah Shillito 43
Thomas E. 40
Wm. E. 43
Rosenberg, Dora Morrow 88
M. C. 88
Rucker, Aurelia C. 15
Joseph 15
Russell, Annie 53
L. H. 53
Louis Henry 53
M. A. 53
Sadie 53
Russum, Marion W. 84
Talmadge W. 84
Rutledge, P. S. 73
Sadler, James H. W. 46
Sassard, Anna Rosa (Miss)
50
Henrietta (Mrs.) 51
John H. (Capt.) 43
N. T. 65
Schroeder, Augustus B. 86
Eliza C. Brooks 86
J. V. 86
John V. 86
Scott, Sallie 84
Seal, J. O. 11
L. V. 11
Lavonia R. 54
Livonia L. 54
Mary Livonia 54
Rosa 54
Sallie Sue 11
T. C. 54
Thomas C. 54
Willie May 54
Selleck, Frederick W. 49
Sharp, Carl P. 68
Celestea E. 50
Eunice 67

Sharp (cont.)
Frances 50
Frances Elizabeth
(Miss) 90
J. B. 67
Jas. B. 67
M. J. 67
Mary J. 67
Matilda 50
Sharpe, Elise B. 90
James William 79
John H. 79
Shaw, B. L. 1
Ernest 1
Lillian 1
Shehan, Jeremiah 37
Sherard, Tabitha M. 64
William C. 64
Shillito, Andrew W. 60
James 30, 31
Jennie 31
M. M. 30, 31
Sarah Lydia 30
Shrine, Anna Ethridge 77
C. 77
Shuman, Sarah Haigler 8
Shurnat, Mary Louise 90
Sign, Henry Hemphill 6
Henry R. 6
J. W. 60
Jimmie Elwell 60
John W. 60
John W. (Jr.) 60
Julia 60
Julia Shillito 60
Lewis W. 60
Simmons, Annie Ruth 82
Bessie 83
Bessie Wilson 83
Cassie 78
David 82
E. Alice Millford 56
Fred D. 82
J. H. 56
J. T. 78
Jas. H. 45
Mary 45
Mattie F. Wade 82
R. Y. 83
Robert Y. 83
Sallie 82
Sammie M. 45
W. D. 82
William C. 82
William T. 82
Simpson, Deney 12
J. Earnest 1, 3
James Vernon 86
Jason L. 2
Ralph Edwin 92
W. W. (Mr.) 92
W. W. (Mrs.) 92
Sitton, Clarence Edwin
23
Harriet D. 23
James L. 23
Small, Emilie Washington
16
Eva Enverdale 15
Louisa 15
Mary Irwin 15
Smith, A. H. 65
A. M. 29
A. W. 14
Annie 85
Aug. W. 14
Augustus 14
Augustus M. 14

Smith (cont.)
Augustus Marshall 14, 81
B. C. 56
Belle 29
Bennie A. 85
Edward Harden 65
Ernest 14
Fannie J. (Mrs.) 39
Frances J. 38
Henry Gillespie 65
I. 29
Ione 29
J. A. 56, 65
J. Allen 55, 65
J. Allen (Jr.) 65
Lewis Wardlaw 14
Louisa Jane Allen 29
M. B. 65
M. N. 14
Mabel C. Upchurch 29
Mamie Lou 29
Margaret 14, 90
Mary B. Hardin 65
Mary Noble 14
Rebecca C. Cothran 55
Roselie Ella 14
Sarah L. 29
Sarah M. 14
Sarah Margaret Wardlaw 14
W. D. 85
W. J. 29
W Joel 29
Walter David 85
William (Capt.) 39
Willie Seal 54
Wm. (Capt.) 38
Sondley, Annie B. 63
D. R. 35
L. P. 63
M. F. 35
Mary Frances 35
Richard 63
Virginia C. 35
Sorrow, A. H. 72
Belle 1
F. D. 72
J. W. 72
James Homer 75
L. M. 72
N. 72
Parks E. 1
Speed, A. O. 7
Althea 7
E. F. 7
Ezekiel 7
Fannie Ferguson 66
Howard Owens 7
Julia Baker 7
P. B. 7
Preston Brooks 7
W. R. 7
William Terril 66
Spierin, Elizabeth Shauklin 20
Julia Josephine 20
Patrick (Mrs.) 20
Thomas Piercy 20
Sproull, Charles Wm. 40
Susan Claudia 40
Sprouse, Clifton 81
Cora Lee 92
Florence Wilson 87
I. E. 78
Idona 81
J. L. 87
Lizzie 84

Sprouse (cont.)
R. G. 78
William R. 92
Stallings, Thos. A. 84
Stark, Ann Miller 7
Starr, M. J. 48
Mary J. E. 48
R. C. 48
Stephens, Edith L. Leach 5
Mary E. 5
W. G. 5
W. T. 5
William G. 5
Stevenson, Andrew 70
Annie Evelyn 80
Eliza A. 24
Esther Fleming 89
H. O. 43
J. A. 90
J. C. 25
James C. 25
Lulie Reid 90
M. R. 80
Mary A. 25
Mary R. 80
Nancy 25
Rebecca 25
Robert M. 89
Susan 25
Thomas 25
W. A. 80
William 25, 43, 70
Wm. Oscar (2nd Lt.) 80
Stewart, Raford E. 87
W. A. 59
Stokes, John T. 12
Verna Clinkscale 12
Stone, Carl (Jr.) 96
Charles 91
Louessa Stewart 59
Strain, Elizabeth Ann 40
Mary 34
Robert 34
Strawhorn, Fannie 91
Frances Inez 86
I. M. 86
J. M. (Mr.) 77
J. M. (Mrs.) 77
J. W. 91
James M. 77
Janie Sharpe 86
Lemuel Kenneth 91
M. J. 91
S. M. 91
Sarah E. 86
W. T. 86
Sullivan, F. A. 53
T. A. 53
Swetenburg, B. F. 59
George Carroll 58
M. E. 59
Mary J. Milford 59
Syfan, A. B. (also see Syfan, A. R.) 32
A. R. (also see Syfan, A. B.) 32
Dollie 32
E. M. 32
Frances K. 32
G. W. 32, 74
G. W. (Sr.) 32
Geo. W. 32
George Whitfield 32
K. H. 32
Katie H. 32
M. B. 90
M. E. 32

Syfan (cont.)
Mamie Cochran 90
Mary 32
Mary Eliza 32
Nina A. Isaacs 74
Taggart, Hal 77
James 77
Lesly Harris 33
Mary 33
Mary Holcomb 77
Moses 33
Moses (Sr.) 33
William S. 9
Tarrington, G. E. 57
Orson Rawley 57
S. T. 57
Teal, Thomas 50
Templeton, Eliza Ann Giles 45
James Patterson 45
Sarah M. (Mrs.) 45
W. L. (Dr.) (also see Templeton, W. T.) 45
W. T. (Dr.) (also see Templeton, W. L.) 45
William Augustus 45
Tennent, Charles 36
Luvinia 36
Martha 36
Susanah V. 36
William 36
Wm. 36
Wm. (Rev.) 36
Thomas, David Walter 13
E. Annie 13
E. H. 48
Elizabeth H. 48
Elizabeth H. K. 13
Elizabeth Hamilton Kirk 13
Grace Allerton 13
Henry Crowell 49
Henry Walter 48
James W. (Dr.) 13
James Walter 13
Jas. Walter 13
John Archer 45
Lora 12
Margaret B. 12
Mary Cheatham 13
P. (Capt.) 13
Robert Walter 48
T. W. 48
Thomas Walter 13, 48
V. D. 12
Willie 13
Thomson, C. B. 66
Eliza 27
Frances Bradley 27
J. C. 66
J. W. 50
Jack 50
James Calvert 66
John Allen 45
Lucy C. (Mrs.) 45
Margaret Martha 27
Ninian 27
R. O. 2
S. E. 2
Samuel Goode (D.D.S.) 61
Sarah A. 50
Sarah Amanda 50
Thomas 27, 50
Thomas P. 27
Thos. 27

Thomerson, Ben Alexander
    87
  J. H. 87
Thorton, J. F. 6
Tilman, Edward 80
  Kitty Calhoun 80
Timmons, Betty J. 8
Toland, Mary 29
Togno, Joseph 49
Tribble, Irene W. 86
  J. W. (Mr.) 86
  J. W. (Mrs.) 86
  James William 86
  William Radford 86
Trowbridge, Anna Branch
    34
  J. W. 34
  Jessie 34
  Julia Cecelia 34
Turman, Frank L. 77
  J. Y. 77
  James Milton 77
  Julia M. 77
  O. 77
  Ora 77
Tusten, A. A. 38
  Agnes Ann 38
  Alice 38
  Ames H. 38
  Argrove A. 38
  Edna M. 38
  H. T. 38
  J. H. 38
  James Thomas 38
  Jonnie 38
Uldrick, B. A. 85
  C. C. (Mr.) 91
  C. C. (Mrs.) 91
  Carrie 91
  H. H. 75
  J. E. 52
  J. J. 52
  J. T. 75
  J. Y. 52
  Jane Y. (Mrs.) 52
  Joseph P. 52
  Julia M. 76
  L. T. 63
  M. J. 52, 76
  M. L. 63
  Mamie L. 63
  Marhta Jane Winn 76
  O. M. 85
  R. S. 91
  Ruby Mae (Miss) 75
  S. M. 52
  T. F. 75
  U. B. 76
  W. B. 52, 76
Vose, Carsten 42
  Louisa R. Burn 42
Wadkins, Maggie (Miss)
    (also see Watkins)
    65
Walker, Lizzie C. 64
Wardlaw, A. B. 30, 48
  Andrew Bowie 30
  Ann A. Louisa 22
  Charles C. 30
  Clara A. 30
  D. L. 22, 47
  David A. 30
  David Lewis 14, 46, 47
  Edward Robert 46
  Edward Tilman 46
  Eliza 30
  Eliza Bowie 30
  Eliza L. 30

Elizabeth A. 22
George Allen 47
Hannah 22, 46
Hiram Tilman 46
I. 46
Ivy 46
J. J. (Dr.) 46
James 22, 46
James A. 30
James Alfred 30
James Frances 22
James H. 22
James Joseph 46
James Witherspoon 46
Jas. A. 30
Joseph J. (Dr.) 46
Joseph James (Dr.) 46
Joseph Walter 30
Lewis Alfred (1st Sgt.)
  46
Lewis Joseph 30
Lucea Garvey 14
Lula L. 69
M. A. 46
M. I. 69
Marnie 30
Mary 30
Mary Ann 46
Mary Caroline 22
Mary Elizabeth 22
Nannie Amelia White 48
Robert H. 30
Robert Henry 30
Rosa 30
S. E. 30
S. R. 22
Sally E. 30
Sarah Allen 14
Sarah Margaret 14
Sarah R. 22
Sarah R. (Mrs.) 47
T. Perrin 30
Thornwell 46
W. A. 46
W. P. 69
William Alfred 46
Waters, Virgil M. 66
Watkins, J. A. 65
  Maggie (Miss) (also
    see Wadkins) 65
  Nannie F. L. 65
  Sallie M. 65
Watson, Henry 85
Watt, Janet 22
  John 22
  Sam. I. 29
  Samuel 22
Welsh, Dale Barksdale 66
Westfield, Charley S. 50
  Edward 50
  John Livingston 50
  Sarah J. 50
  Sarah L. 50
  V. E. 50
  Virginia E. 50
  William Walker 50
Whaley, J. H. (Mr.) 86
  J. H. (Mrs.) 86
Wharey, Elizabeth King 88
  Thomas (Rev.) 88
Wham, J. I. O. 4
  Ida 4
  J. M. 4
  John T. 4
  Mary Helen 4
White, Arianah E. (Miss)
    49
  Celia Chalmers 33

White (cont.)
  Charles Smith 63
  Edna H. 80
  Eleanor Dean 59
  Ellen Scott 63
  F. E. (Mrs.) 64
  George 63, 70
  J. H. (Rev.) 59
  James R. 89
  John 48, 63
  John Bonah (M. D.)
    70
  Julia C. (Miss) 50
  L. W. 70
  Lambert Jones 70
  Leonard W. 70
  Leonard Waller 70
  Lucy 48, 63
  Lucy Agnes 48
  M. H. 70
  Marguerite 89
  Mary H. 70
  Mary Helen Jones 70
  N. W. 89
  Nannie Amelia 48
  Nelle 70
  Sarah Eliza 63
  Shirley B. 87
  T. A. 33
  T. S. 89
  Vemmie 2
  Wm. H. 80
  Wm. Henry (Capt.) 48
Wideman, Martha Ann 40
Wier, A Lythgoe 37
  Alexr. Sloan 37
  Ann Martin 17
  J. A. 37, 38
  Joel C. 38
  John 17
  John Alex 38
  Kate 38
  Leila May 38
  Lillie P. 38
  Margaret 17
  S. B. (also see Wier,
    S. M.) 37, 38
  S. M. (also see Wier,
    S. B.) 37
  Susan Benson 38
  Susan Evaline 37
Wilkes, L. R. 85
  Louise Reid 85
  R. C. 85
Wilkinson, Claude P. 88
  Julian Mann 88
Williams, A. A. 37
  A. H. 4
  Blanche 2
  C. M. 2
  E. A. 4
  E. Alvin 4
  E. E. 4
  Eddie Alvin (Jr.) 4
  James Edward 4
  Leila 4
  Lucile 2
  R. L. 4
  Sarah C. 4
Willis, A. H. 2
  Ben S. 2
  Japhos R. 2
  S. L. 2
  Samuel A. 2
Willson, Alax.r 26
  Anna Eliza 31
  Emity Augusta 79
  I. B. 79

Willson (cont.)
J. R. (Capt.) 31
J. R. F. 76
James Samuel 31
John 26
John (Jr.) 26
John (Sr.) 26
John R. 31
L. R. 79
M. Edwin 78
Mary 31
Robert W. 26
William A. 74
Wilson, Alma J. 87
Anna 24
Birdie 76
Clarience Edwin 24
Courtney A. 62
Dionysius A. (2nd Lt.) 28
E. L. 62
E. R. (Mr.) 67
E. R. (Mrs.) 67
Edwin Lindsay 52
Elizabeth 20, 26, 33
Emma H. (Miss) 52
Ernest O. 75
F. A. 28
F. M. 66
Fannie E. Willis 2
Frank A. 76
G. E. 78
G. T. 24
George T. 24
Grace 24
Henry Latimer 80
Herbert A. 58
Hugh 12, 74
J. A. 12
J. L. 1
J. Lowrie (Rev.) 64
J. S. (Mrs.) 21
James S. 17, 21
Jennie Bone 75
Jno. A. (Mr.) 80
Jno. A. (Mrs.) 80
John 26
John A. 80
John B. (Sgt.) 76
John H. 45
John R. 2
John R. (Jr.) 82
Joseph D. (M. D.) 59
Kathern M. 82
L. W. 62
LeRoy C. 54
Leroy J. 24
Lillie Brooks 62
Linda Higgason 12
Lizzie 24
M. J. 58
Macklin P. 28
Marie 87
Mary (Mrs.) 12
Mary Elizabeth 52
Mary Josephine 58
Mary Virginia 52
Matthew 20, 33
Matthew Harvey 76
R. C. 62
R. Evelina 54
Rachel Ramona 82
Richard C. 62
Robert Wesly 12
Ruth E. 87
S. A. 28
Samuel Link 80
Sarah A. 76

Wilson (cont.)
Sarah Abigail 62
Sarah Elizabeth 24
Sarah M. 76
Sarah U. 24
Susan A. 24
Susan Ann 28
Susan V. 17
Susie May 24
Thomas Alexander 17
W. C. 62
W. J. 87
W. R. 2
W. S. 58
Wade H. 76
Wallace G. 82
William 52
William D. 31
William J. 58
William R. 2
William Samuel 58
Willie Coogler 62
Z. E. 66
Winn, A. 44, 57
Adolphie 73
Andrew 44, 46
Daniel F. 44
Edward F. M. 44
H. M. 42
Henry M. 42
J. B. 73
J. D. 73
J. D. (Mr.) 73
J. D. (Mrs.) 73
J. P. 73
Jefferson D. 73
Jessie 73
Luana 42
M. 57
M. A. 46, 73
M. E. 73
Martha 44
Mary A. C. 46
Mary Elizabeth 73
Mary R. 42
Nannie R. 73
Parthena C. 46
Paul D. 73
R. H. 46
R. L. 73
Robert L. 73
Robt. H. 46
Witherspoon, James H. (Col.) 46
Jane D. 46
Woolbright, E. G. 10
E. M. 4
E. P. 4
Euna Ethelene 4
Jack (Jr.) 10
S. J. 10
Woodhurst, Claud H. 87
E. F. 79
Eva Marguerite 79
J. A. (Mr.) 87
J. A. (Mrs.) 87
James Preston 87
R. S. 79
Word, Robert 38
Wosmansky, C. B. 75
E. Alice Millford 56
Florence 75
J. C. 56
John Charles 56
L. O. 75
Lucile 75
Wright, J. W. 81
James W. 81

Wright (cont.)
Lety C. 81
W. T. 81
Yarbrough, Mary 17
William 17
Yoder, Clyde Ernest 89
Young, C. F. 10
Charlie 10
Doris 10
F. E. 10
James E. 9
John T. 65
Zeigler, Benie 68
Georgia Caroline 69
Henrietta Emory 69
Jennie 68
L. A. 68, 69
Lavinia A. 68
M. G. 68, 69
Martin Govan 68
Samuel Jacob 69
Zimmerman, Catherine 21
Virginia Gamorell 7
Walter S. 7

www.ingramcontent.com/pod-product-compliance
Lightning Source LLC
Chambersburg PA
CBHW070929270326
41927CB00011B/2777